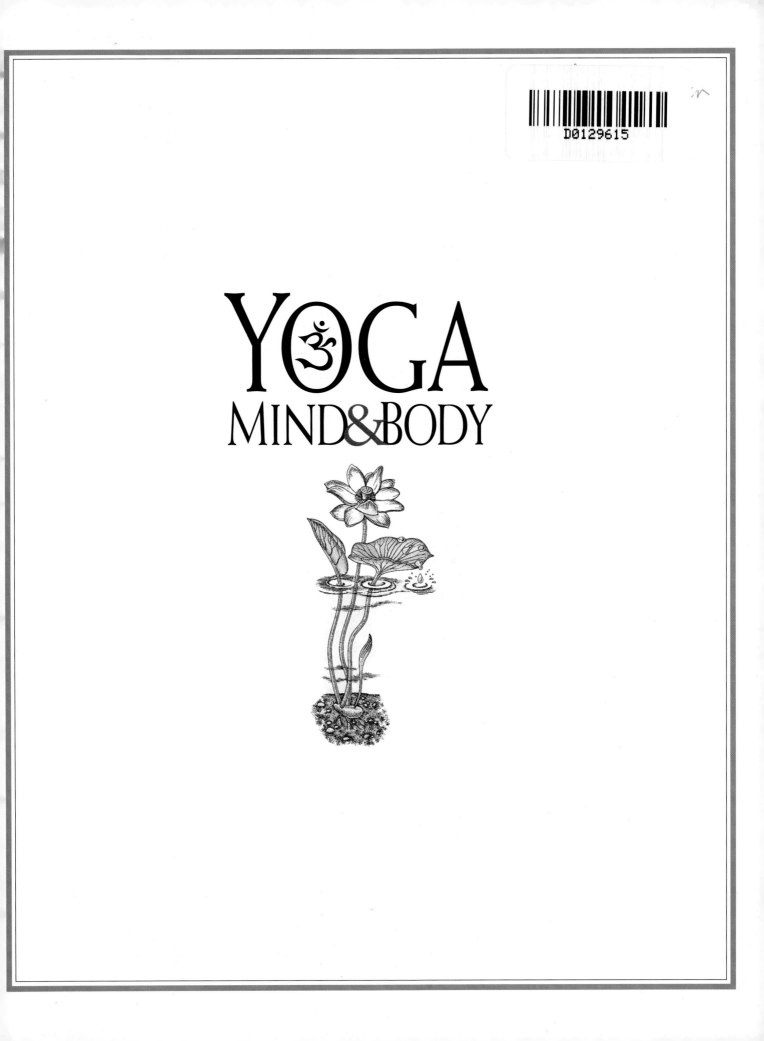

YOGA
MIND & BODY

YOGA
MIND&BODY

SIVANANDA YOGA VEDANTA CENTRE

FIREFLY BOOKS

DK

A DORLING KINDERSLEY BOOK

PUBLISHER'S NOTE: The views and opinions expressed in this book
are those of the Sivananda Yoga Vedanta Centre

PROJECT EDITORS Ian Whitelaw, Irene Lyford
PROJECT ART EDITORS Colin Walton, Ted Kinsey
COMPUTER PAGE MAKEUP Mark Bracey
MANAGING EDITOR Mary-Clare Jerram
MANAGING ART EDITOR Amanda Lunn
PRODUCTION Michelle Thomas

First Canadian edition 1996
Published in Canada by Firefly Books Ltd.
3680 Victoria Park Avenue, Willowdale, Ontario. M2H3K1

First published in Great Britain in 1996
by Dorling Kindersley Limited
9 Henrietta Street London WC2E 8PS

CANADIAN CATALOGUING IN PUBLICATION DATA

Main entry under title:

Yoga mind & body

Includes index.
ISBN 1-55209-013-2

1. Yoga, Hatha. I. Sivananda Yoga Vedanta Centre.
II. Title: Yoga mind and body.

RA781.7.Y64 1996   613.7'046   C95-933255-3

Text film output by Optigraph, Great Britain • Color reproduction by Colourscan, Singapore • Printed in Italy by A. Mondadori Editore, Verona

CONTENTS

WHAT IS YOGA?

Yoga is a way of life, an integrated system of education for the body, mind, and inner spirit. This art of right living was perfected and practiced in India thousands of years ago but, since Yoga deals with universal truths, its teachings are as valid today as they were in ancient times. Yoga is a practical aid, not a religion, and its techniques may be practiced by Buddhists, Jews, Christians, Muslims, Hindus, and atheists alike. Yoga is union with all.

THE SYNTHESIS OF YOGA

Over the centuries, four different paths of Yoga (Karma, Jnana, Bhakti, and Raja) have developed. They are often likened to four branches of a banyan, or peeple, tree, which puts down roots from its branches and appears to be growing down to Earth from Heaven. Since we each have our own personality, we may prefer one path to another, but a one-sided development is not recommended, since it can lead to an imbalance in the personality. The whole person – heart, intellect, and hand – should be developed simultaneously, so a synthesis of the four main paths is recommended. It is best to have one basic sadhana (spiritual practice) or preferred path, but to draw from the techniques of the others as well.

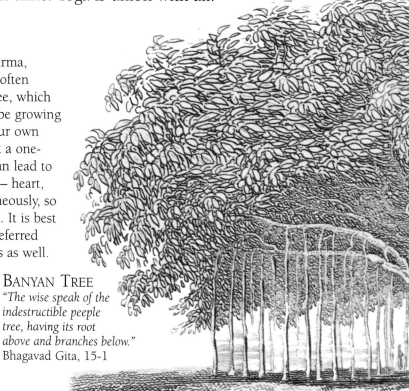

ACTIVE PATH - *KARMA YOGA*

Karma Yoga is selfless service, the path by which the mind is most quickly purified and its limits transcended. The Karma Yogi works hard, both physically and mentally. He or she seeks to eliminate the ego and its attachments, to serve humanity without expecting reward, and to see unity in diversity. This enables the Yogi to tune to the one underlying divine essence that dwells within all beings. Karma Yoga is most suitable for people who have an active temperament. It involves working in the world and giving of oneself, but working on a spiritual level.

BANYAN TREE
"The wise speak of the indestructible peeple tree, having its root above and branches below."
Bhagavad Gita, 15-1

WORK AS WORSHIP
Many people complain that they have insufficient time for their practice; they are too busy, or are disinclined to do asanas or to meditate. In Karma Yoga, the work itself is the practice, if performed with the right mental attitude.

PHILOSOPHICAL PATH - *JNANA YOGA*

This philosophical or intellectual approach to spiritual evolution describes the world as an illusion. Using the two powerful intellectual techniques of Viveka (discrimination) and Vairagya (dispassion), the veils of illusion, or Maya, are lifted. Jnana Yoga is usually regarded as the most difficult of the four paths of Yoga. This path demands a sharp mind and an unclouded intellect.

ANCIENT SCRIPTURES
The philosophy, or Vedanta, of Jnana Yoga was originally written in books made of palm leaves.

DEVOTIONAL PATH - BHAKTI YOGA

Bhakti Yoga tends to appeal to people who are emotional by nature. Since the emotions cannot be endlessly repressed, Bhakti Yoga teaches techniques for their sublimation. Through various practices, such as chanting, prayer, and the repetition of mantra (sacred formulae), emotional energy is channeled into devotion, turning anger, hatred, and jealousy in a positive direction. Emotional love is changed into pure divine love. The Bhakta tries to see God in all.

PRAYER POSE
Namaskar, or the Prayer pose, signifies the joining of the individual soul with the divine soul. This concept of union with the divine through devotion, or bhakti, is found in all of the world's great religions.

SCIENTIFIC PATH - RAJA YOGA

We each possess vast mental and psychic resources that lie virtually untapped below the surface of the conscious mind. To release this latent potential, Raja Yoga prescribes a psychological approach, based on a practical system of concentration and control of the mind. Right conduct, a healthy body and steady posture, breath regulation, and withdrawal of the senses are recommended to achieve this. Only if this foundation is firm can the superstructure of concentration and meditation succeed. Hatha Yoga is a form of Raja Yoga that emphasizes asanas (postures) and pranayama (breath control).

ASANAS
Steady postures form an important element in the practice of Raja Yoga.

THE EIGHT STEPS OF RAJA YOGA

By observing their own thoughts, scientifically and objectively, the ancient Yogis studied the many obstacles to bringing the mind under conscious control. The sage Patanjali compiled their findings in the Raja Yoga Sutras, a text that describes the inner workings of the mind, and also provides an eight-step (ashtanga) blueprint for controlling the restless mind and enjoying lasting peace.

8. SAMADHI

7. DHYANA

6. DHARANA

5. PRATYAHARA

4. PRANAYAMA

3. ASANAS

2. NIYAMAS

1. YAMAS

WHAT ARE THE STEPS?

1 Yamas (abstentions) – truth, nonviolence, control of sexual energy, nonstealing, noncovetousness.
2 Niyamas (observances) – austerities, purity, contentment, study, surrender of the ego.
3 Asanas – steady poses.
4 Pranayama – control of vital energy.
5 Pratyahara – withdrawal of the senses.
6 Dharana – concentration of the mind.
7 Dhyana – meditation. 8 Samadhi – the superconscious state.

THE THREE BODIES

Most of us might question whether the body has a soul. But the Yogi would say definitively, "I am a soul that has taken a body." Yoga philosophy sees the body as a vehicle for the soul in its journey toward enlightenment, and goes on to discuss not just one body, but three bodies, each more subtle than the one before.

1. PHYSICAL BODY

In Sanskrit, the physical body is known as the Annamaya kosha, or food sheath. This visible dense body is born, grows, changes, decays, and then dies, the components returning to the earth and the food cycle. Seeing the attention that the Yogi pays to the physical body, observers might conclude that Yoga is a glorification of the body, but the aim is to bring the physical body under the conscious control of the mind. Both can then be used for higher spiritual pursuits. Proper care of the physical body is necessary if any work is to be done.

Emotions have their roots in the Karmic impressions of past lives, which percolate through the astral body into the physical body

△ FOOD SHEATH
"Just as a man casts off worn-out clothes and puts on new ones, so also the embodied Self casts off worn-out bodies…"
Bhagavad Gita, 2-22

• 1. FOOD SHEATH
The physical body is made of one layer, known as the food sheath.

8

3. CAUSAL BODY

Called the "karana sharira" in Sanskrit, the causal body is also known as the seed body. Just as a seed or a bulb contains within itself an exact blueprint of the plant it will produce, so the causal body stores subtle impressions in the form of Karma. These subtle impressions control the formation and growth of the other two bodies, and determine every aspect of the next birth. At the time of death, both the causal and astral bodies (which remain together) separate from the physical body.

KARMIC SEEDS △
Just as a bulb contains instructions for growth, so the seed body stores the Karma, subtle impressions of everything that has happened to you in this life and in past lives. Karma is not fate, destiny, or luck, but the result of your own past actions.

• 3. BLISS SHEATH
The causal or seed body has only one layer, the Anandamaya kosha, or bliss sheath, in which the experiences of happiness and joy reside.

• 2C. INTELLECTUAL SHEATH
The Vijnanamaya kosha of the astral body is the decision-making faculty. The ego – the sense of who I think I am – resides here.

• 2B. MENTAL SHEATH
The second layer, the Manamaya kosha, is where thought, doubt, exhilaration, depression, and delusion are experienced.

• 2A. PRANIC SHEATH
In the first layer of the astral body, called the Pranamaya kosha, we experience such sensations as heat and cold, hunger and thirst.

2. ASTRAL BODY

Every living being has an astral body. This is connected to the physical body by a subtle thread along which vital currents pass. When this cord is cut, the astral body departs and the body dies. It is composed of three layers:
A. PRANIC SHEATH More subtle than the food sheath, but similar in form, it is often spoken of as the etheric double. It is made up of 72,000 nadis, or astral tubes, through which prana, or vital energy, flows.
B. MENTAL SHEATH Comprising the automatic mind, as well as the instinctive and subconscious regions, this is where we carry on the automatic functions of our daily lives. It is very jumpy by nature, as it is constantly bombarded by input from the five senses.
C. INTELLECTUAL SHEATH The intellect controls and guides the automatic mind. Discrimination and decision making take place here and pass down to the more gross sheaths.

AJNA CHAKRA ▷
The chakras, where the astral tubes meet, are found in the pranic sheath. The Ajna chakra, the energy center also referred to as the "third eye," is situated between the eyebrows.

THE YOGIC PATH TO INNER PEACE

THE OM SYMBOL

Yoga is a life of self discipline based on the tenets of "simple living and high thinking." To the ancient Yogis, the body was seen as a vehicle for the soul, and this is a useful metaphor in the modern context. Just as a car requires a lubricating system, a battery, a cooling system, the proper fuel, and a responsible driver behind the wheel, so the body has certain needs if it is to function smoothly.

PROPER EXERCISE - *ASANAS*

In Yoga, the physical exercises, called "asanas" (see pp.14–105), are nonviolent and provide a gentle stretching that acts to lubricate the joints, muscles, ligaments, tendons, and other parts of the body. Asanas help to tone the nervous system, improve circulation, release tension, and increase flexibility. When performed in a slow and relaxed manner, they are designed to develop more than just the physical body. They also broaden the mental faculties and enhance the spiritual capabilities. Asanas make up the third limb, or step, in the Raja Yoga system.

△ THE CRESCENT MOON
This is a good example of a backward-bending asana. Practice helps to maintain and increase the flexibility of the spine.

YOGIC BREATHING - *PRANAYAMA*

Deep breathing helps to cleanse and nourish the physical body. As you inhale fully, you are supplying an abundance of oxygen, an element that is essential to every cell in the body. As you exhale, the waste products are being expelled (see pp.108–9). Breathing also helps to connect the body to its battery, the solar plexus, where tremendous potential energy is stored. When tapped through specific Yogic breathing techniques (pranayama), this vital energy, or prana, is released for physical and mental rejuvenation (see pp.110–113).

◁ CHAKRAS & NADIS
There are 72,000 nadis crisscrossing the astral body. The point where a number of nadis cross is called a chakra. Pranayama cleanses and strengthens the nadis and chakras.

PROPER RELAXATION

When the body and mind are continually overworked and stressed, their natural efficiency diminishes. Rest and relaxation are nature's ways of giving the body a chance to recharge. Like the radiator of a car, they cool down the system. Yogic methods (see pp.118–121) retrain the mind and muscles to relax completely.

FOOD FOR HEALTH ▷
This simple, natural, and easily digested dish is an excellent source of nutrients.

VEGETARIAN DIET

A meat-free diet enables the body to obtain the maximum benefit from food, air, water, and sunlight. The Yogic diet (see pp.124–151) consists of foods that are easily digested and promote good health. As well as being simple, natural, and wholesome, it takes into account the subtle effect that food has on the mind and on the astral body. Followers of a Yogic diet find themselves attaining a high standard of health, a keen intellect, and serenity of mind.

POSITIVE THINKING AND MEDITATION

Just as any vehicle requires an intelligent driver, so the body needs a balanced mind that can stay in control. Regular meditation (see p.156–61) will help you achieve this; your mind will become clearer and more focused, and your ability to concentrate will improve. Positive thinking (see p.154–5) will purify the intellect, and you will begin to experience wisdom and inner peace.

MEDITATION TOOLS △
A japa mala (string of 108 beads) and a candle are among the objects that will help you in your meditation practice.

PROPER EXERCISE

"Asanas are treated of in the first place, as they form the first stage of Hatha Yoga. One should practice asanas that make one firm, free of diseases, and light of limb."

Hatha Yoga Pradipika, 1-19

WHAT IS PROPER EXERCISE?

There are many types of physical exercise, but the Yogic system of asanas (a Sanskrit word meaning "steady pose") is the most complete, benefiting far more than just the physical body. The asanas emphasize deep breathing, relaxed movements, and mental concentration.

THE ASANAS

Asanas are designed to promote a state of mental and physical well-being, or good health. This may be defined as the condition that is experienced when all the organs function efficiently under the intelligent control of the mind. Asanas have an extraordinary capacity to overhaul, rejuvenate, and bring the entire system into a state of balance. Although they are performed by the physical body, asanas also have profound effects on the astral body.

ASANA BENEFITS

▶ **PHYSICAL BENEFITS:** It is often said that "You are as young as your spine." Asanas initially focus on increasing and maintaining flexibility of the spine, toning and rejuvenating the nervous system. The gentle stretching, twisting, and bending movements bring flexibility to the other joints and muscles of the body, as well as massaging the glands and organs. Circulation is also improved, ensuring a rich supply of nutrients and oxygen to all the cells of the body.
▶ **MENTAL BENEFITS:** Steady postures free the mind from disturbances caused by physical movement, promoting steadiness of mind, balanced emotions, and an improved outlook on life.
▶ **PRANIC BENEFITS:** Asanas work in much the same way as acupuncture or shiatsu, but the Yogic system of pranic balancing is more subtle. To gain the benefit, you must practice asanas regularly over a period of time, but once you feel the benefits, they will last longer. The different poses put pressure on various points, purifying and strengthening the nadis.

PHYSICAL BENEFITS •
With regular practice, asanas encourage all parts of the body to work more efficiently.

MENTAL BENEFITS •
Many people believe that asanas were originally designed as concentration exercises to help improve the mind's capacity to meditate.

PRANIC BENEFITS •
Asanas increase pranic energy, which can be utilized for awakening the spiritual potential.

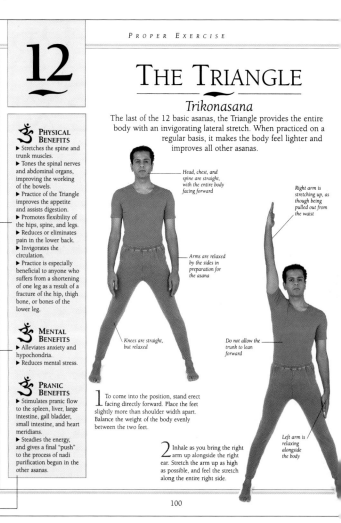

12

🕉 **PHYSICAL BENEFITS**
▶ Stretches the spine and trunk muscles.
▶ Tones the spinal nerves and abdominal organs, improving the working of the bowels.
▶ Practice of the Triangle improves the appetite and assists digestion.
▶ Promotes flexibility of the hips, spine, and legs.
▶ Reduces or eliminates pain in the lower back.
▶ Invigorates the circulation.
▶ Practice is especially beneficial to anyone who suffers from a shortening of one leg as a result of a fracture of the hip, thigh bone, or bones of the lower leg.

🕉 **MENTAL BENEFITS**
▶ Alleviates anxiety and hypochondria.
▶ Reduces mental stress.

🕉 **PRANIC BENEFITS**
▶ Stimulates pranic flow to the spleen, liver, large intestine, gall bladder, small intestine, and heart meridians.
▶ Steadies the energy, and gives a final "push" to the process of nadi purification begun in the other asanas.

THE TRIANGLE
Trikonasana
The last of the 12 basic asanas, the Triangle provides the entire body with an invigorating lateral stretch. When practiced on a regular basis, it makes the body feel lighter and improves all other asanas.

Head, chest, and spine are straight, with the entire body facing forward

Right arm is stretching up, as though being pulled out from the waist

Arms are relaxed by the sides in preparation for the asana

Knees are straight, but relaxed

Do not allow the trunk to lean forward

Left arm is relaxing alongside the body

1 To come into the position, stand erect facing directly forward. Place the feet slightly more than shoulder width apart. Balance the weight of the body evenly between the two feet.

2 Inhale as you bring the right arm up alongside the right ear. Stretch the arm up as high as possible, and feel the stretch along the entire right side.

100

WHO CAN DO YOGA?
Yoga can be practiced by anyone, regardless of age, sex, or physical ability. It will enhance your studies, reduce stress, and help you to enjoy your free time. However, if you suffer from any specific medical condition, it is best to check with your doctor before taking up asana practice. Yoga should not be seen as a substitute for a medical prescription.

ASANAS & VARIATIONS

There are 12 basic asanas. They are numbered 1–12, and are shown in the order in which you should perform them. They are demonstrated by Shambu (below). Once you have mastered these, start including the variations and more advanced positions, which Amba demonstrates (right). Other positions are shown by Rhadika.

PROPER EXERCISE

TRIANGLE *Variations*

In its various permutations, the Triangle ensures a thorough lateral stretch to all parts of the body, promoting elasticity of the spine and helping to maintain a youthful posture.

VARIATION 1

This asana introduces a forward bend to the basic Triangle, stretching the body in a slightly different way.

Elbows are kept straight as the arms are lifted

Head and spine are kept in a straight line

Hands are clasped together with the fingers loosely interwoven

Knees are straight, but do not try to tighten them

Left foot is turned out so that the two heels are now at a 90° angle to each other

1 Standing with the feet a little more than shoulder

2 Exhale and bend forward, bringing the forehead toward the left knee. Lift the arms as high as ... the position for at least 10 seconds. ... to 1 minute. Inhale as you stand ... position, and repeat on right side.

VARIATION 3

This is a further variation in which the body is stretched in a deep lunge position. Practice on both sides.

Keep the body centered; do not lean to one side as you bend the knee

Right foot is flat on the floor

1 With your feet a bit more than shoulder width apart, turn your left toes outward and bend the left knee. Bring your arms parallel to the floor at shoulder level.

The body forms a straight line from the foot to the fingertips

The left knee is directly over the left foot

Elbows are straight

2 Place your left hand flat on the floor inside the left foot. Bring your right arm up next to your ear. Hold for 10 seconds, increasing to 1 minute.

2 Exhale as you bring the forehead toward the floor just inside the left foot. Hold for at least 10 seconds, breathing gently. Gradually increase to 1 minute. Return to the starting position, and repeat by lunging to the right.

Left knee is bent, with the thigh parallel to the floor

... knee is straight with the ... flat on the floor, do not ... the foot to rotate inward

Head and chest are held erect

Arms and shoulders are in a straight line

VARIATION 4

This apparently simple variation involves considerable chest and shoulder flexibility. Watch the alignment of arms and chest.

1 Stand with the feet a little more than shoulder width apart. Raise the arms until they are held straight out from the shoulders.

Legs are straight

2 Twisting from the hips, place the right hand flat on the floor outside the left foot. Align the body so that shoulders, chest, and arms form one straight line. Look up at the left hand. Hold for at least 10 seconds, and then repeat on the other side.

Right shoulder is directly over the right hand

103

THE TRIANGLE

Stretches the muscles of the side of the body from the feet to the fingers

MAJOR BENEFIT

The Triangle gives an excellent, and complete, lateral stretch to the entire body. All the muscles are positively affected, especially those along the outer side of the body. These include the muscles of the ankles, legs, hips, and arms.

Right arm is straight and alongside the right ear

Eyes should be fixed straight ahead

COMMON PROBLEMS

▸ One or both knees are bent.
▸ Body is twisted forward or back.
▸ Upper elbow is bent.
▸ Head is dropped forward.
▸ Weight is mainly on one leg, rather than being evenly distributed.
▸ Weight is placed against the thigh by the lower hand.
▸ Eyes are looking downward.

Do not allow the body to twist

Left hand is resting gently on the outside of the left leg; imagine trying to grasp the ankle

Hand is placing weight against the thigh

3 Exhale as you bend to the ... left. Slide the left hand ... the left leg as far as ... sible. Breathing regularly, ... the position for at ... st 30 seconds, and ... dually increase to ... ninute. Return to ... center and repeat ... the other side. ... form this basic ... angle 2–5 times ... each side.

101

◁ PROPER SUPERVISION

This book is meant to be an introduction to Yoga. It is best to be supervised by a teacher who is qualified and can correct and inspire you. Your teacher should understand the physical workings of the body and should teach from direct experience. When looking for a teacher, ask whether he or she practices on a regular basis.

HOW TO USE THE PROGRAM

The 12 basic asanas, plus the Sun Salutation, should be practised in every asana session. If you are a beginner, you should focus on these until you have mastered them. They will prepare you to proceed to the variations. Each time that you stretch in one direction, you will be asked to stretch in the opposite direction, so do not skip the counter-poses or the relaxation. Begin each session with at least 5 minutes of relaxation, end with 10 minutes of relaxation, and relax between asanas. Exercise slowly, and always practice the asanas in the order in which they are shown. Do not force your body into positions that it is not ready to perform. Correct breathing forms an important part of many asanas, but when there are no specific breathing instructions you should breathe naturally.

Clothes should be made of cotton

Loose clothes allow free movement

Asanas are best done with bare feet

WHAT TO WEAR ▷

To permit freedom of movement, clothing should be loose and comfortable. Cotton fabric allows the body to breathe better than synthetic materials.

PREPARATORY EXERCISES

Since a relaxed body and mind function more efficiently, it is of the utmost importance to prepare yourself for the asanas with at least 5 minutes of complete relaxation. If you are cold when in the Corpse pose or Easy Sitting position, cover yourself with a blanket to keep warm.

THE CORPSE POSE
Sarvasana

Lie flat on your back with your arms and legs apart and eyes closed. To ensure that there is no tension in the body, shake out the shoulders. Slowly roll the head from side to side once or twice, bringing one ear to the floor, and then the other. Bring the head back to the center and focus the mind on the breath.

Mind is focused on the breath

Breathing is through the nose

Abdomen rises and falls with inhalation and exhalation

Feet are at least 1½ft (50cm) apart

Back is flat on the floor

Arms are at an angle of approximately 45° to the body

Hands are relaxed with the palms facing upward

Toes are falling out to the sides

Legs are straight but not tense

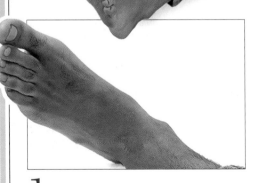

1 Placing your feet about 1½ft (50cm) apart, with your legs straight but relaxed, allow your toes to fall outward.

2 With your arms at an angle of about 45° to your body, relax your hands, palms upward, on the floor.

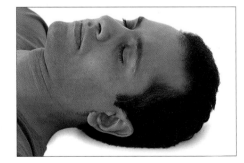

3 Close your eyes, breathe through your nose, and concentrate on the breathing rather than on external events.

EASY SITTING POSITION
Sukasana

In preparation for the breathing exercises or the exercises for the eyes and the neck, adopt a simple cross-legged position. This posture provides a very firm and stable base for the body, as well as serving to keep the energy centered.

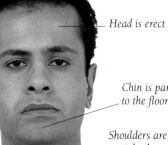

Head is erect

Chin is parallel to the floor

Shoulders are straight, but relaxed

Back is straight

Back of the hand rests on the knee

Tips of thumb and index finger are joined in the classical Chin Mudra position (see below)

Legs are crossed

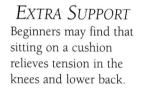

EXTRA SUPPORT
Beginners may find that sitting on a cushion relieves tension in the knees and lower back.

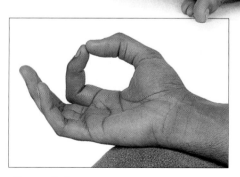

CHIN MUDRA
For this classical position, bring the tips of the thumb and index finger together.

ALTERNATIVE HAND POSITION
Clasp the hands by gently interlocking your fingers. Rest the hands in your lap.

SECOND ALTERNATIVE
Place one hand on top of the other in your lap, with the palms upward.

EYE EXERCISES

Like any other part of the body, the eye muscles need exercise; modern social conditions require far less eye movement than living in a natural environment. Yogic eye exercises help to keep the muscles strong and active.

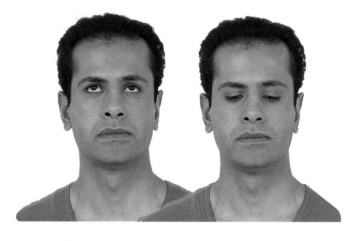

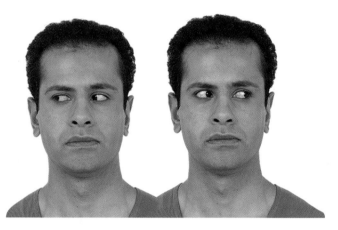

1 ◁ Keeping the back and neck straight and the head still, look up as high as possible, and then look down. Repeat this exercise at least 10 times. Close and relax the eyes for about 30 seconds before moving on to the next exercise.

2 △ Keeping the eyes wide open, look as far to the right as possible, and then to the left. Repeat the exercise at least 10 times, then close and relax the eyes for 30 seconds.

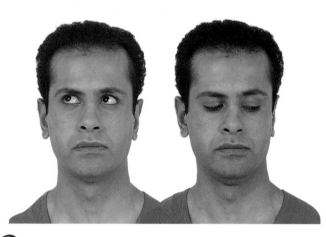

3 △ Move the eyes diagonally by looking from the upper right-hand corner to the lower left and back again. Do this 10 times. Repeat the exercise by looking from the top left corner to the bottom right. Close and relax the eyes.

4 ◁ Make wide circles with your eyes by rolling them clockwise. Beginning slowly, gradually increase the speed until you are moving the eyes as fast as possible. Perform at least 10 circles. Close the eyes for a moment, and then repeat the exercise counterclockwise. Close and relax the eyes.

RELAXING THE EYES

Warm hands cupped over your eyes provide heat and darkness to soothe and relax them after the exercises.

1 After the eye exercises, rub your hands together vigorously until the friction between them warms up the palms.

2 Gently cup the hands over your closed eyes, without touching the eyelids. Hold them there for about 30 seconds.

NECK ROLLS

Most people seem to hold most of their tension in the neck, shoulders, and upper back. Performing a series of neck rolls before beginning the asanas will help to release some of this blocked energy. Start in the Easy Sitting position (see p.17), with your back straight and your chest erect. Only the head and neck should move; the back and shoulders should remain steady.

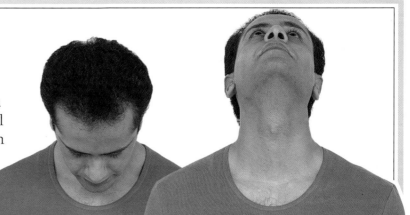

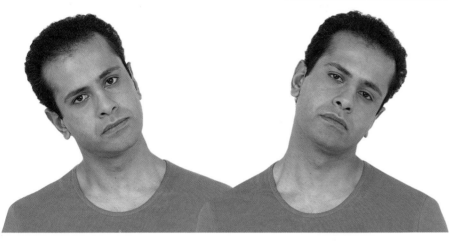

1 △ Hang the head forward, and rest the chin on the chest for a few moments. Feel the back of the neck stretching. Now drop the head back as far as possible, as if trying to touch your spine with the back of your head. Repeat the exercise 5–10 times.

2 ◁ Without twisting the head, bring the right ear down toward the right shoulder. Hold it for a moment, bring the head to the center and then stretch to the left. Repeat 5–10 times in each direction.

3 ▷ Without moving the shoulders, turn your head to look over your right shoulder as far as possible. Return to the center and then look over the left shoulder. Repeat 5–10 times on each side.

4 ▽ Drop the chin to the chest and rotate the head clockwise 2 or 3 times. Bring the head to the center and start again, performing 2 or 3 times in a counterclockwise direction.

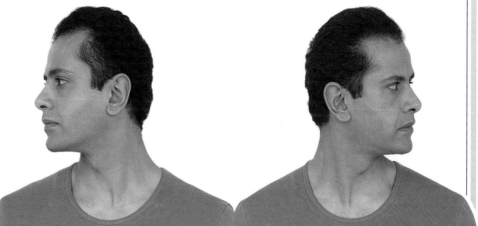

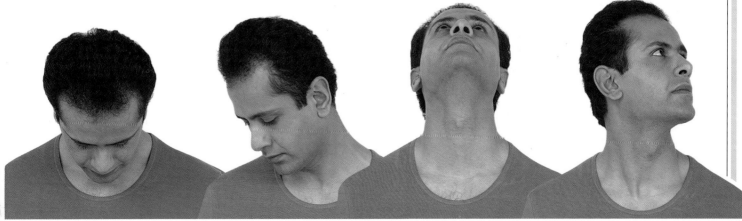

THE SUN SALUTATION

Surya Namaskar

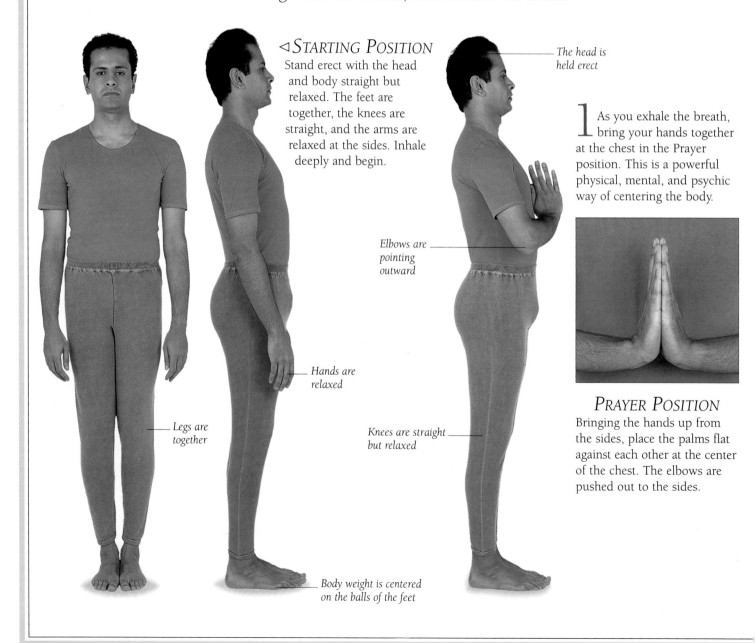

All sessions of Yoga asanas begin with the Surya Namaskar, or Sun Salutation. This excellent warm-up exercise consists of a sequence of 12 positions that move the spine in various ways and promote flexibility in the limbs. It is of special benefit to beginners, to stiff people, and to the elderly, since it helps the body to gain flexibility. It also regulates the breath, and focuses the mind.

◁ *STARTING POSITION*
Stand erect with the head and body straight but relaxed. The feet are together, the knees are straight, and the arms are relaxed at the sides. Inhale deeply and begin.

The head is held erect

1 As you exhale the breath, bring your hands together at the chest in the Prayer position. This is a powerful physical, mental, and psychic way of centering the body.

Elbows are pointing outward

Hands are relaxed

Legs are together

Knees are straight but relaxed

Body weight is centered on the balls of the feet

PRAYER POSITION
Bringing the hands up from the sides, place the palms flat against each other at the center of the chest. The elbows are pushed out to the sides.

Elbows are straight

Arms are alongside the ears

Hold the head back slightly

2 ◁ Inhale and stretch your arms up over your head. Arch your body backward, keeping the arms alongside the ears, and the knees straight.

Arch the hips forward

Keep the knees straight

Make sure that the hips stay as high as possible

Fingers and toes are in a straight line

Head is tucked in toward knees

Hands are as flat on the floor as possible

3 △ Exhale as you bend forward and bring the hands down to the floor next to the feet. If you cannot put your hands on the floor with the knees straight, bend the knees slightly.

Head is held up

Lift the hips

Top of the foot is flat on the floor

Keep the hands on the floor next to the feet

4 △ Without moving your hands, inhale and stretch the right leg back as far as possible. Drop the right knee to the floor and then stretch the head up.

Do not lift the hips

Do not allow the head to drop

Keep the body straight

5 ▷ Retaining the breath, bring the left leg back and place the left foot next to the right, with the toes pointing forward. Your body should now be in a straight line, in a posture often known as the push-up position.

Hips are kept up

Forehead is brought down to the floor

Knees are on the floor

Chest is on the floor

6 Exhaling, drop the knees straight down to the floor. Keep the hips up. Without rocking the body backward, bring the chest straight down to the floor between the hands. Bring the forehead to the floor; beginners may place the chin on the floor if this is difficult to do.

Head is stretched back

Shoulders are relaxed

7 Inhale as you slide the body forward until the hips are on the floor. Arch the chest up and bring the head back into the Cobra pose (see pp.64–5). Do not move the hands. The elbows are slightly bent, with the shoulders down and back, so that there is no tension in the neck or shoulder area.

Knees are straight, with the legs parallel to each other

Elbows are slightly bent

Hands are flat on the floor with the fingers together

Hips are on the floor

Hips are raised as high as possible

Head is between the arms, so that you are looking at your feet

8 Exhale as you tuck the toes under. Without allowing the hands or feet to move from their positions, bring the hips up. Push the heels toward the floor and keep the knees straight. Drop the head down between the arms. This is often referred to as the Inverted V pose.

Hands remain flat on the floor

Heels are stretching toward the floor

Look upward

9 Inhale and bring the right foot forward between the hands so that the fingers and toes form a straight line. Drop the left knee to the floor and stretch the head up. This is the same as the position in Step 4.

Back knee is on the floor

The front foot remains between the hands

Hips are as high as possible

Head is in toward the knees

10 ▷ Without moving the hands, exhale as you bring the left foot forward next to the right foot. The forehead is down toward the knees. This is the same position as that shown in Step 3.

Fingers and toes are in a straight line

Arms are stretched up alongside the ears

Elbows are straight

Head is stretched back

The chest and entire thorax region are arching forward

Keep the head and neck relaxed but erect

Body is straight

Hips are pushed forward

11 Inhale as you slowly reach the arms forward and then stretch them up over the head. With the arms alongside the ears, and the weight centered on the balls of the feet, give a complete backward bend to the body. This is the same position as in Step 2.

Knees are straight

12 ▷ Exhale as you stand upright and bring your arms down alongside your body, returning to the starting position. You are now ready to begin the next Sun Salutation cycle. In the steps shown here, you are asked to lead with the right leg, but for the next cycle, you should lead with the left leg.

Hands are relaxed by the sides

THE SUN SALUTATION

Breathing Sequence

Technically, Surya Namaskar is not an asana, but a series of gentle flowing movements synchronized with the breath. Once you have learned the positions of the Sun Salutation, it is important to tune them to a rhythmic breathing pattern. Try to do 6–12 cycles of the Sun Salutation every day.

12 Exhale as you return to the starting position, feet together and hands by the sides. Inhale deeply, and return to Step 1.

11 Inhale as you stretch up and arch back, with your head back and your arms up alongside the ears.

10 Exhale and bring the other foot forward. Straighten the knees and bring the forehead down and in toward the legs.

9 Inhale and bring the right foot forward between the hands. Drop the back knee to the floor and look up. (Bring the left leg forward in the next sequence.)

8 Exhale and, without moving your hands or feet, bring the hips up as high as possible into the Inverted "V" position.

7 Inhale, slide the hips forward, and arch the head and chest up into the Cobra pose (see pp.64–5).

1 Standing upright, exhale as you bring the palms together at the chest in the Prayer position.

2 Inhale and stretch the arms up over the head alongside the ears. Arch back from the waist, pushing your hips forward and stretching the head back.

3 Exhaling, bring the hands down to the floor on each side of the feet so that the tips of the fingers and toes form a straight line. Tuck your head in toward the knees as far as possible.

4 Inhale as you stretch the right leg back as far as possible, and drop the right knee to the floor. (On the next sequence you will stretch the left leg back.)

5 Holding the breath, bring the other leg back and straighten the body into the push-up position.

6 Exhale and bend the knees. Place the knees, chest, and forehead on the floor.

1

THE HEADSTAND

Sirshasana

The Headstand, one of the most powerful postures, is often referred to as the King of the Asanas because of its numerous mental and physical benefits. Many rightly see it as a panacea for all human ailments. If you have only a short time to practice, and want to maximize benefits, do the Headstand. In this inverted position, at least 90 percent of the body weight should rest on the elbows. Hardly any pressure should be taken by the head or neck.

PHYSICAL BENEFITS

▶ Gives the heart a well-deserved rest, as gravity helps to return venous blood to the heart.
▶ Regular practice helps to strengthen the respiratory system and the circulation, keeping them flexible and slowing down the rate of breathing and the heartbeat when at rest.
▶ Refreshes the entire body through deep breathing.
▶ Brings a rich supply of nutrients to the brain, spine, and nervous system, rejuvenating the whole body.
▶ Relieves varicose veins.

MENTAL BENEFITS

▶ Increases memory, concentration, and intellectual capacity.
▶ Enhances the sensory faculties.

PRANIC BENEFITS

▶ "He who practices the Headstand for three hours daily conquers time." – *Yoga Tatwa Upanishad.*
▶ Sublimates sexual drive by transmuting seminal energy into Ojas-Shakti.

STARTING POSITION: CHILD'S POSE

Begin by sitting on the heels with the forehead resting on the floor. Place the hands, palms upward, on either side of the feet. If you find this impossible, place your fists on top of each other and rest your forehead on them. Allow the body to relax and sink down into this position.

Back and neck are relaxed

Toes point backward

Forehead is on the floor

1 ▽ Sit up on the heels and begin to come into the Headstand by making a firm foundation to support the body. Clasp each elbow with the opposite hand to ensure that the elbows are the correct distance apart.

Hold each elbow firmly with the opposite hand

Elbows are directly beneath shoulders

*Forearms form a
triangular base to
support the body*

*Fingers are
loosely
interlocked*

*Elbows are
beneath the
shoulders*

2 △ Release the elbows without moving them. Clasp the hands together on the floor in front of your face to form a firm tripod position.

3 ▷ Without moving the arms, place the top of the head on the floor, with the back of the head firmly against the clasped hands.

*Hands are clasped around
the back of the head*

PREPARATORY EXERCISE: THE DOLPHIN

The Dolphin is recommended even when you are able to do the Headstand, since it will strengthen the arms and shoulders and enable you to hold the position correctly for longer periods.

Hips are up

*Keep the head
up as high as
possible*

1 ▷ Follow Steps 1 and 2 of the Headstand. Now, keeping the head up and without moving the feet away from the arms, straighten the legs so that hips rise to form an inverted "V."

*Feel the
weight on
the elbows*

2 ▷ Rock the body forward so that the chin comes over the hands and then in front of them.

Chin is forward

*Raise the
hips high*

*Knees must be
kept straight*

3 ▷ Push the body backward as far as possible. Rock back and forth 8–10 times before relaxing into the Child's pose. Repeat this process 3–4 times daily to strengthen the arms and shoulders.

*Keep the knees
straight*

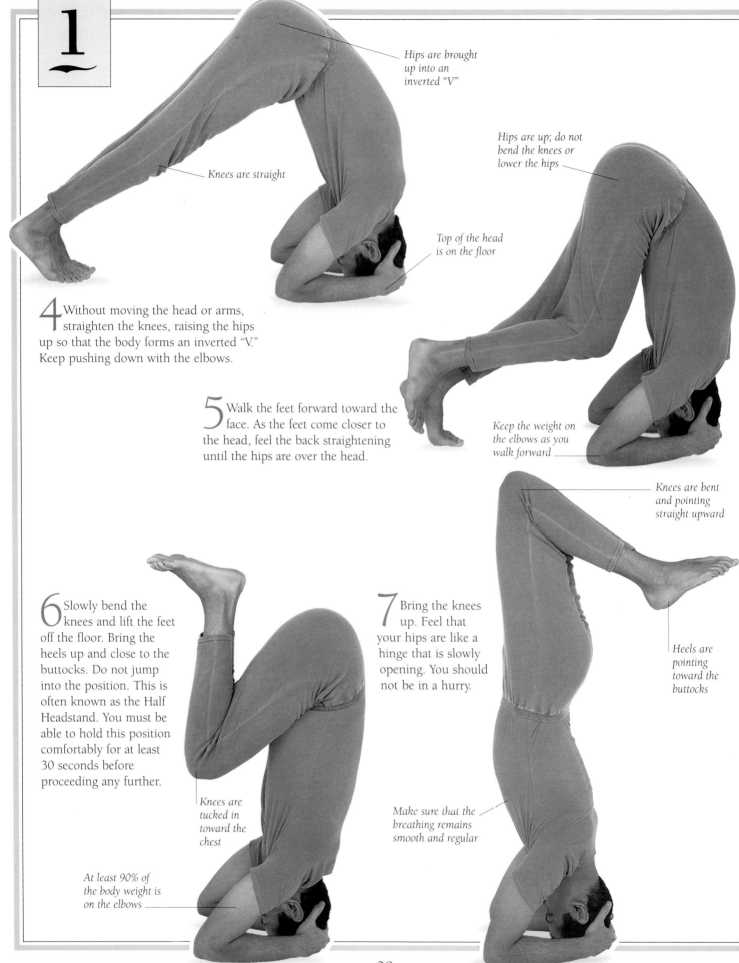

1

Hips are brought up into an inverted "V"

Knees are straight

Hips are up; do not bend the knees or lower the hips

Top of the head is on the floor

4 Without moving the head or arms, straighten the knees, raising the hips up so that the body forms an inverted "V." Keep pushing down with the elbows.

5 Walk the feet forward toward the face. As the feet come closer to the head, feel the back straightening until the hips are over the head.

Keep the weight on the elbows as you walk forward

Knees are bent and pointing straight upward

6 Slowly bend the knees and lift the feet off the floor. Bring the heels up and close to the buttocks. Do not jump into the position. This is often known as the Half Headstand. You must be able to hold this position comfortably for at least 30 seconds before proceeding any further.

7 Bring the knees up. Feel that your hips are like a hinge that is slowly opening. You should not be in a hurry.

Heels are pointing toward the buttocks

Knees are tucked in toward the chest

Make sure that the breathing remains smooth and regular

At least 90% of the body weight is on the elbows

8 Slowly straighten the knees, bringing the feet up toward the ceiling. Try to hold the position for at least 30 seconds, gradually increasing to 3 minutes. Keep the weight on the elbows. Before you are too tired, come out of the position by first bending the knees, then the hips. Bring the feet to the floor and then drop your hips back onto the heels. Relax in the Child's pose (see p.26) for at least a minute before raising the head. Then relax in the Corpse pose (see p.16) before continuing.

Heels stretch up toward the ceiling

Knees are straight

The entire body from head to heels is in a straight line

Keep the abdominal muscles tightened so that the back doesn't overarch or the hips drop backward

Breathing is very slow and relaxed

Rib cage is tucked in

Keep the weight on the elbows, with almost no weight on the head or neck

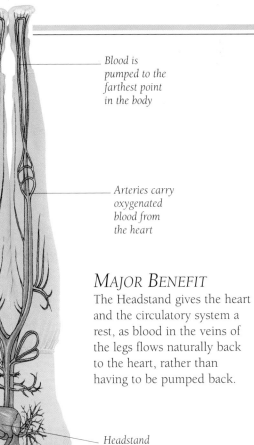

Blood is pumped to the farthest point in the body

Arteries carry oxygenated blood from the heart

Major Benefit
The Headstand gives the heart and the circulatory system a rest, as blood in the veins of the legs flows naturally back to the heart, rather than having to be pumped back.

Headstand relaxes the heart

Common Problems

▶ Legs are dropping back and are not together.

▶ Knees are bent.

▶ Weight is being placed on the head, rather than on the elbows.

▶ Shoulders are hunched.

▶ Back is arched.

▶ Elbows are too far apart.

▶ Caution: You should not attempt the Headstand if you have high blood pressure, are more than four months pregnant, have glaucoma or similar eye problems, have recently suffered whiplash or a similar injury, or if you have been advised against this form of exercise.

Legs are bent and apart

Too much weight is placed on the head

HEADSTAND *Variations*

STARTING POSITION

Once you have mastered the basic Headstand, and can hold it comfortably for at least 3 minutes, try some variations from that position. All start from the Headstand. They are designed to improve flexibility, concentration, and balance. They also strengthen the muscles of the back and shoulders, and give an extra stretch to the legs and thighs.

◁ONE LEG TO FLOOR

Keeping one leg up, exhale and lower the other leg until the foot is 2in (5cm) from the floor. Inhale as you raise the leg up again. Repeat 2–3 times on each side.

BOTH LEGS TO FLOOR ▽

Keeping the legs together, exhale as you lower them, stopping 2in (5cm) from the floor. Feel as though the hips are pulling back, to counterbalance the weight of the legs.

Knees are kept straight

Foot is lowered to within 2in (5cm) of the floor

Knees are straight

Keep the elbows firmly pushed onto the floor

Hips are up and back

Feet are lowered to 2in (5cm) from the floor

Knees are straight

LEGS TO FRONT AND BACK

Keeping the knees straight, bring one leg forward and the other back. Stretch the heels out away from each other. Change legs, reversing the position several times. Finish by bringing your legs back to the starting position and straightening the body before continuing with the asanas.

Back remains straight

Body is relaxed, with weight on the elbows

Knees are straight

Breathing is smooth and slow

Arms and shoulders are relaxed

LEGS OUT TO SIDES ▷

Keeping the knees straight, bring the legs out to the sides as far as possible, without dropping them forward. Be aware of keeping the back straight as you practice this, and all the Headstand variations. Do not allow the spine to arch backward too much.

Keep the feet together, but relaxed

◁ HANDS FLAT

From the basic Headstand position, take a deep breath, shift the weight slightly to the left, and quickly bring the palm of the right hand flat on the floor in front of you. Repeat with the other hand. This should not be attempted by beginners. Do not hold for too long, since pressure is put on the head and neck.

Heels are up toward the ceiling

Knees are straight

ARMS EXTENDED ▷

From the Hands Flat position, inhale and shift the weight slightly to one side. Straighten one elbow, and place the hand palm upward on the floor. Repeat with the other hand. You may only be able to hold this position briefly. This variation maximizes the benefits for concentration and balance.

Abdominal muscles keep the body straight

Top of the head is on the floor

Elbows are straight

Palms are flat on the floor

Palms face upward

Do not allow the top of the head to rotate forward

THE SCORPION
Vrichikasana

The Scorpion, which is an advanced position, promotes balance and brings harmony to the body and the mind. Before attempting this pose, you should feel secure in the Headstand and be able to hold it for at least 3 minutes.

STARTING POSITION

2 Release the interlocked fingers slowly, and move your hands apart, bringing them to lie flat on the floor on either side of the head. Feel confident in this position before continuing. Inhale deeply as you pause, before trying the next step.

1 Starting from the Headstand (see pp.26–9), bend the knees and begin to bring the feet slowly down toward the head. Arch the entire body backward, being sure to keep the weight of the body on the elbows.

Knees are bent

Back is arched

Weight of the body rests on the elbows

Back continues to arch

Forearms are as parallel to each other as possible

Palms are flat on the floor

VARIATION 1

From the Scorpion, straighten the legs, keeping the weight on the elbows. This pose demands more strength, but less upper back flexibility.

Knees are straight

Lower back is strongly arched

VARIATION 2 ▷

From the Scorpion, arch the back further and bring the feet onto the head. This requires great flexibility of the entire spine.

Entire back is arched

Head is lifted

Legs are relaxed and parallel to each other

3 Keeping the back arched, lift the head as you bring the shoulders back into a position directly above the elbows. You are now in the Scorpion position. It requires a good deal of concentration, strength, and upper back flexibility. Hold the position only for as long as you feel comfortable.

Feet are relaxed

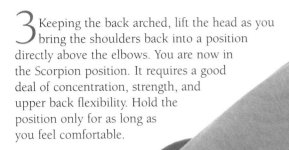

Head is raised up as high as possible

Shoulders are directly over the elbows to provide support for the body

Very little weight is placed on the hands, but they do provide additional balance

STABLE BASE

In the Scorpion position, keep the hands apart and the head up. The weight of the body rests on the elbows, while the hands provide extra stability.

2

THE SHOULDERSTAND

Sarvangasana

The Shoulderstand is said to benefit the whole body; its Sanskrit name comes from "sarva," meaning "all parts." When practicing the Shoulderstand, you may have the impression that the body is being bent backward, but the Shoulderstand is actually a forward-bending exercise, with the main stretch taking place in the shoulder, neck, and upper back regions. For the Shoulderstand and asanas following in this series, you will need at least 1ft (30cm) between the fingertips and any wall when your arms are fully extended.

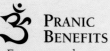

ॐ PHYSICAL BENEFITS

▶ Presses the chin to the throat, bringing a rich blood supply to the area.
▶ Massages the thyroid gland, bringing it to its proper level of activity.
▶ Centralizes the blood supply in the spinal column and stretches the spine, helping to keep it strong and elastic.
▶ As most of the body is inverted, it prevents venous blood stagnating in the lower limbs and encourages circulation, helping to relieve varicose veins.
▶ Encourages deep abdominal breathing, massaging the heart and lung regions.

ॐ MENTAL BENEFITS

▶ Relieves lethargy and mental sluggishness.
▶ Helps cure insomnia and depression.

ॐ PRANIC BENEFITS

▶ Focuses on the psychic energy center, Vishuddha chakra, in the throat region.
▶ Stimulates pranic flow in the stomach, small intestine, urinary and gall bladders, pericardium and kidney meridians.

PREPARATORY EXERCISES

All these exercises are performed lying on the back. Their purpose is to strengthen the muscles of the abdomen and lower back gradually, preparing them for the Shoulderstand and other asanas.

STARTING POSITION

Lying flat on the floor, bring the legs together and the hands flat on the floor next to the sides, keeping the back flat against the floor. Hold the chin toward the chest, so that the back of the neck stays flat.

Legs are together

Arms are flat on the floor at the sides

Toes are pointed back toward the head

SINGLE LEG RAISES ▷

Inhale as you raise the right leg. Exhale and lower it. Try to tune the movement of the leg to the breath. It should take about the same amount of time to exhale as to lower the leg. Repeat with the left leg. Practice this exercise 2–5 times on each leg.

Palms are flat on the floor

Back is flat on the floor

Chin is tucked toward the chest

1 Lying flat on your back, bring the feet together and stretch the arms behind your head to make sure that you have enough space. Return the arms to the floor next to the hips, and place the hands flat on the floor.

Back is flat on the floor

Chin is kept down toward the chest

Legs are together

Arms are next to the body with the palms facing downward

Shoulders are relaxed

LEG STRETCH

From the Single Leg Raise, keep the leg up. Reach up with both hands and grasp the leg as high up as you can without lifting the head or back. Gently stretch the leg toward the head. Repeat with the other leg.

Do not hold the leg too high since it will force you to bend the knee and you will lose the benefit of the exercise

Keep the head and neck on the floor

Both knees are straight

Leg is pulled back toward the head

Knees remain straight

HEAD RAISE ▷

Keeping hold of the leg, bring the head up toward the knee. Return the head to the floor, release the leg, and gently lower it to the floor. Repeat on the other side.

Stationary leg stays flat on floor

Keep the feet together as you raise the legs

Chin is tucked toward the chest

Keep the back flat on the floor

◁ DOUBLE LEG RAISES

Inhale as you raise both legs, keeping them together. Keep your back flat and the chin forward, since arching the back will put undue strain on it. Exhale as you slowly lower the legs, pushing the back flat against the floor. Repeat at least 5–10 times. If you have a very weak back, practice Single Leg Raises until the muscles are strong enough for this exercise.

2 Keeping the back, head, and neck on the floor, inhale as you raise both legs, bringing them up at a right angle to your body. Place the hands on the buttocks, and prepare to lift the body.

Legs are straight and together

Trunk remains on the floor

Hands will come onto the buttocks

Head remains on the floor

Feet and calf muscles are relaxed

3 Begin to push the body up gently by walking the hands down the back. Continue this gradual movement until you are resting on the shoulders. Never move into the position suddenly.

The closer the hands are to the shoulders, the straighter the back will be

If the leg muscles start to cramp, bend the knees slightly for a few seconds to relieve the tension

Move your weight gradually onto the shoulders

Elbows are as close together as possible

4 Straighten the back as much as possible, and hold for at least 30 seconds, gradually increasing to 3 minutes. To come out of the position, beginners should lower the feet to a 45° angle over the head, place the hands flat on the floor behind the back, gradually unroll the body, and relax. Intermediate students can proceed to the other asanas in the Shoulderstand Cycle (see pp.46–7) before relaxing.

Legs should be straight, but relaxed

Thyroid gland

Thyroid cartilage

Thyroid gland

Trachea

FRONT VIEW OF THROAT

MAJOR BENEFIT

This position strengthens and balances the function of the thyroid, which supervises the other glands, promotes the growth and development of the body, regulates metabolism and heat production, and controls the heart rate.

HAND POSITION

Hands are flat on the back, with the fingers pointing in toward the spine. From time to time, readjust the body by moving the hands a little closer to the shoulders, and the elbows slightly closer to each other.

Back is as straight as possible

COMMON PROBLEMS

▶ Elbows are too far apart or are unevenly positioned.

▶ Head and/or neck are twisted to one side.

▶ Hips are rotated outward, throwing the entire body off balance.

▶ Body is off-center, leaning to one side.

▶ Legs are separated.

▶ Knees are bent.

▶ Breath is held or erratic.

▶ Feet and/or calves are tensed.

▶ Hands are unevenly positioned.

Hands are not evenly positioned on the back

Lift up from the base of the neck

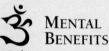

3

THE PLOW
Halasana

Keeping the spine flexible is the key
to maintaining a youthful body.
The Plow, an extreme forward-
bending exercise, promotes both
strength and flexibility in all the
regions of the back and neck.

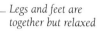

PHYSICAL BENEFITS

▶ Stimulates the spinal
nerves and brings an
increased blood supply
to the region, nourishing
many of the essential
internal organs.
▶ Improves the blood
circulation in general.
▶ Releases tension from
the cervical (upper back)
and shoulder regions.
▶ Massages the internal
organs; indigestion and
constipation are relieved
and can eventually be
eliminated completely.

MENTAL BENEFITS

▶ Relieves insomnia
and restless sleep.
▶ Enhances
physical and
mental relaxation.
▶ Helps to develop
mental poise and
inner balance.

PRANIC BENEFITS

▶ Brings a greater
concentration of prana
to the neck, the cervical
(upper back) region, and
the throat.
▶ Stimulates the
stomach, spleen, small
intestine, heart, liver, gall
bladder, and kidney
nadis (acupuncture
meridians).

*Legs and feet are
together but relaxed*

1 After holding the Shoulderstand for between
30 seconds and 3 minutes, depending on
your expertise, you are ready to come into the
Plow. If you are a beginner, you can relax in the
Corpse pose (see p.16) before continuing.

*Back is as straight
as possible*

Chin is pressing on the throat

*Hands are as close to
the shoulders as possible*

*Hands are flat on
the floor with the
palms downward
and fingers together*

*Arms are
parallel to
each other*

*Keep the hands
on the back*

*Knees are
straight*

*Lower the legs
slowly, with
control*

2 From the Shoulderstand, keeping
the legs together, exhale as you
slowly lower both feet to the floor
behind the head. If you are unable to
bring the toes to the floor, lower them
as far as possible.

3 If you can bring the toes to the floor, place the hands flat on the ground behind the back, palms downward. Tuck the toes in toward the head and gently push the heels toward the floor. Hold for at least 30 seconds, breathing gently. Gradually increase to 2 minutes.

Lumbar region is stretched

Circulation is increased in the thoracic region

Stress is released from the cervical region

MAJOR BENEFIT

All regions of the spine and back muscles are stretched, but the Plow benefits the muscles of the upper back and the neck particularly, since the position releases stress from these areas.

Keep the hips as high as possible

Legs, feet, and thighs are together

Toes point toward the head

COMMON PROBLEMS

▶ Knees are bent.

▶ Hands are out to the sides and/or are held with palms upward.

▶ Head and/or neck are twisted.

▶ Legs are skewed to one side.

▶ Hands are not on the floor.

▶ Shoulders are twisted.

▶ Hips and back are not lifting up.

Hands should be on the floor

▶ CAUTION: If the toes do not comfortably reach the floor, keep the hands on the back, supporting the back muscles until they become more flexible.

Roll down vertebra by vertebra

Keep your head on the floor

Use the hands for support

4 To come out of the pose, return to the Shoulderstand, and lower your feet halfway to the floor. Place your palms flat on the floor behind the back, and breathe gently as you roll down slowly with control, keeping your head on the floor. (For Plow variations, see pp.44–5.)

THE BRIDGE

When performed immediately after the Plow, the Bridge acts as a gentle counterpose to complement and enhance the benefits of both the Shoulderstand and the Plow. It assists the body in releasing any tension that may have built up in the thoracic and lumbar regions of the spine while practicing the two previous asanas. Sethu Bandhasana, as the Bridge is called in Sanskrit, is usually practiced as part of each asana session. Two methods of coming into the Bridge are shown here – one for intermediate students and one, in the box below, for beginners.

Calf muscles are relaxed, as are the feet

STARTING POSITION ▷

For intermediate students, the starting position for the Bridge is the Shoulderstand, which should be held for 1–3 minutes before moving on to the Bridge.

Arms are supporting the entire body

Do not allow the knees to bow out to the sides

Feet and legs are parallel

BEGINNERS' METHOD

You should be able to hold the Bridge position comfortably for at least 30 seconds before you attempt any of the Bridge variations (see pp.42–3).

1 Start by lying flat on the back, with your arms at your sides. Bend both knees and bring the feet flat on the floor close to the buttocks.

Feet and legs are apart, but parallel

Arms are on the floor alongside the body

2 Raise the hips, and bring the hands onto the back, placing them in the same way as that shown in the Shoulderstand hand position (see p.37).

Hips and chest are lifting as much as possible

Head, neck, and shoulders are flat on the floor

Feet are flat on the floor; do not come up on your toes

Fingers are pointing in toward the spine with thumbs upward

1 Bend both knees. Slowly, and with full control, begin to arch the body and lower one foot gently to the floor behind the back.

Other foot follows

Lead with one foot first

Fingers are together, pointing toward the spine

Thumbs point toward the chest

COMMON PROBLEMS

▶ Hips are dropped toward the floor.

▶ Knees are bowing out to the sides.

▶ Toes are turning out to the sides.

▶ Head and/or neck are lifting off the floor.

▶ Shoulders are being raised from the floor.

▶ Hand position has changed.

▶ NOTE: One of the greatest benefits of the Bridge is the promotion of suppleness in the wrists. Changing your hand position should be avoided, since it will deprive you of this benefit.

Knees are wide apart

Shoulders and neck are being lifted from the floor

Hips are lifted as high as possible

Chest arches up from the shoulders, which remain on the floor

2 Lower the other leg to the floor. Be sure to keep the hips up, and avoid lifting either the head or the shoulders from the floor. Hold for 30 seconds, breathing deeply. Inhale as you return to the Shoulderstand, and then slowly roll down.

BRIDGE *Variations*

The Bridge is a very simple, but powerful, posture. Once you have mastered it, there are many possible variations that can be tried. Some of these, such as the One Leg Up position shown below, are quite simple and can easily be performed by beginners. This pose forms part of the Shoulderstand Cycle (see pp.46–7).

STARTING POSITION

ONE LEG UP

From the basic Bridge pose, lift one leg and bring the foot up toward the ceiling. This is a simple variation but as you practice it, be sure not to allow the hips to drop. Hold this for at least 10 seconds, gradually increasing to 30 seconds. Lower the leg, and repeat the exercise on the other side.

Foot is lifting up toward the ceiling

Bring the leg toward the head as much as possible

Keep the leg straight

Hips are lifted as high as possible

Thumbs are pointing upward; fingers are in toward the spine

Head, neck, and shoulders are flat on the floor

The other foot remains flat on the floor

BRIDGE *Advanced Variations*

Do not be in a hurry to move on to advanced variations. The simple variations of the Bridge are the most important, and it is these that should be practiced regularly. Even the basic posture will develop greater strength and flexibility in your body, and will help your mind to become more focused. However, as the mind often craves variety, some advanced variations are given here.

Foot is stretching upward, but relaxed

BRIDGE IN HALF LOTUS

Neither this nor the Legs Straight pose should be attempted until you have gained sufficient suppleness in the hips and wrists. The starting position for the Bridge in Half Lotus is the Shoulderstand (see pp.34–7).

1 While in the Shoulderstand position, bend the left knee and place the left foot on the right thigh in the Half Lotus position. If you need to, use the hand to bring the foot as far up the thigh as possible

Foot is as close to the body as possible

2 ▽ With both hands on the back in the Shoulderstand hand position, bend the right knee and gently lower the right foot to the floor. Hold for as long as you feel comfortable. Remaining in Half Lotus, take a deep breath and return to the Shoulderstand. Straighten the leg, and repeat on the other side.

Try to bring the bent leg parallel to the floor, so that the hips do not twist

Chin is tucked into the chest

Keep the hips as high as possible

Come into the position slowly, with control

LEGS STRAIGHT ▷

From the basic Bridge, advanced students can begin to bring the feet and legs together, making sure that the knees do not bow out to the sides. Once you can hold this position, start to straighten the knees little by little, walking the feet away from the body without lowering the hips.

Do not allow the hips to drop

Knees must always be in line with the feet

Fingers are pointing in toward the spine; do not change the hand position

43

PLOW *Variations*

Variations on the Plow greatly increase flexibility in the cervical (upper back) region of the spine. The superficial and deep muscles of the back, shoulders, and arms are also stretched and strengthened. The Plow (see pp.38–9) is the starting position for this series of variations. If you cannot comfortably hold the Plow, or if your feet do not come to the floor, do not attempt them.

STARTING POSITION

KNEES TO SHOULDER

This asana, known as Karna Peedasana, gives a gentle but firm stretch to each side of the spine in turn.

1 Keeping the hands on the back, walk both feet along the floor to the right. Be aware of the opposite (left) shoulder and elbow, making sure that both of them stay firmly on the floor.

2 Bend both knees to the right shoulder. Hold for 10 seconds, gradually increasing to 1 minute. Straighten the knees, walk the feet to the left, and bend the knees to the left shoulder. Return to the center.

Knees are bent and are as close to the floor as possible

Toes remain on the floor

Head is straight and both shoulders are firmly on the floor.

▽ ARMS WRAP

From the Plow position, bend the knees and drop them to the floor on each side of the head. Clasp the hands behind the knees. Hold for at least 10 seconds, gradually increasing to 1 minute.

Tops of the feet are flat on the floor

▽ PALMS FLAT

Only attempt this position when you are able to do the Arms Wrap pose with the knees completely on the floor. From this position, release the hands and bring the arms to the floor behind the back, palms down.

Breathe as you hold the position

Knees are bent and are as close to the floor as possible

Elbows are straight

Knees are tucked in toward the shoulders

Palms are flat on the floor behind the back

FEET APART

From the Palms Flat pose, straighten the knees and walk the feet out to the sides as far as possible, keeping the hands flat on the floor. Hold this position for 10–30 seconds. Keep the knees straight, and stretch the hips toward the head.

Palms remain flat on the floor

Heels are stretching toward the floor

Feet are as wide apart as possible

PRAYER POSITION

From the Feet Apart position, keeping the feet on the floor, bring the hands over the head. Place the palms flat against each other in the traditional Prayer position (see p.20). Hold for 10 seconds, gradually increasing to 1 minute.

Hands are together

Keep the legs straight and as far apart as possible

Elbows are straight

Toes are tucked under, and heels are stretching toward the floor

FEET AND HANDS

From the Prayer position, bring the legs together and bend the knees, dropping them behind the head. Clasp the hands together and bring them to the floor behind the back. This promotes maximum flexibility of the shoulders and upper back.

Fingers are loosely interlocked (or palms down on the floor)

Knees are together and as close to the floor as possible

Feet are together

THE SHOULDERSTAND CYCLE

The Shoulderstand, the Plow, and the Bridge form a group of asanas that should always be done in sequence as a single cycle, usually without relaxing between the different positions. Variations of each basic asana may be inserted in the sequence if you wish. If you feel tired at any point, come into the Corpse pose (see p.16) to relax for a few minutes.

Feet and legs are relaxed

1 Raise the legs and, walking the hands up the back, gently push the body up until you are resting in the Shoulderstand. Hold for 1–3 minutes, breathing normally.

The back is as straight as possible

Chin is resting on the neck

Hands are on the back with the fingers pointing in toward the spine

STARTING AND FINISHING POSITION

Stretch the heel toward the ceiling

7 Inhale as you lift one leg toward the ceiling and stretch it toward the head in the One Leg Up position. Lower the foot to the floor, and repeat with the other leg. Return to Step 1 before rolling down gently.

Do not permit the hips to drop as the leg lifts

Both feet are flat on the floor with feet and knees parallel

Hips are lifting

6 Bring both feet flat on the floor behind the back, into the Bridge position. Stretch the hips up as high as possible, keeping the feet and legs parallel. Hold for 1–3 minutes, breathing normally.

Do not change the hand position

5 To come into the Bridge, bend both knees and, leading with one foot, slowly lower both legs toward the floor behind the back. Do not change your hand position.

46

Both knees are straight

2 From the Shoulderstand, exhale as you bring one foot to the floor behind the head in the Half Plow position. Hold for a few seconds, then raise the leg and repeat with the other leg. This may be done 2–3 times on each side.

Foot is on the floor with toes toward the head

Hands remain on the back

BACK SUPPORT
While in the Shoulderstand position or the Bridge, keep the hands flat on the back, with the fingers pointing in toward the spine, to provide additional support.

3 From the Shoulderstand, exhale as you slowly lower both feet to the floor behind the head into the Plow position. Bring the arms to the floor behind the back with the palms down. Breathe normally as you hold for up to 2 minutes.

Hands are resting on the floor behind the back

Both feet are on the floor with the toes tucked under

Hands return to the back

Inhale as you lift the body

4 From the Plow, support your back with your hands again, and return to the Shoulderstand, as a preparation for coming into the Bridge. Breathe normally while you hold the position.

4

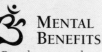

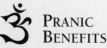

THE FISH
Matsyasana

As the counterposition to the Shoulderstand (see pp.34–7), Matsyasana gives a backward stretch to the cervical, thoracic, and lumbar regions of the spine and expands the chest fully. It is called the Fish because this position fills the lungs with air, improving the ability to float in water.

1 Lying flat on your back, begin by bringing your legs and feet together, keeping the knees straight. Place your hands palms downward beneath the thighs so that you are sitting on them.

Knees are straight

Legs are together

Hands are flat on the floor next to each other

Elbows are under the body as much as possible

Head is resting on the floor

2 Bending the elbows, push them into the floor. Keeping the weight on the elbows, use them to lift the chest until you are sitting halfway up. Do not allow the buttocks or legs to lift.

Chest is lifting off the floor

Feet are together, but relaxed

Knees remain straight

Buttocks are on hands

Weight is on the elbows

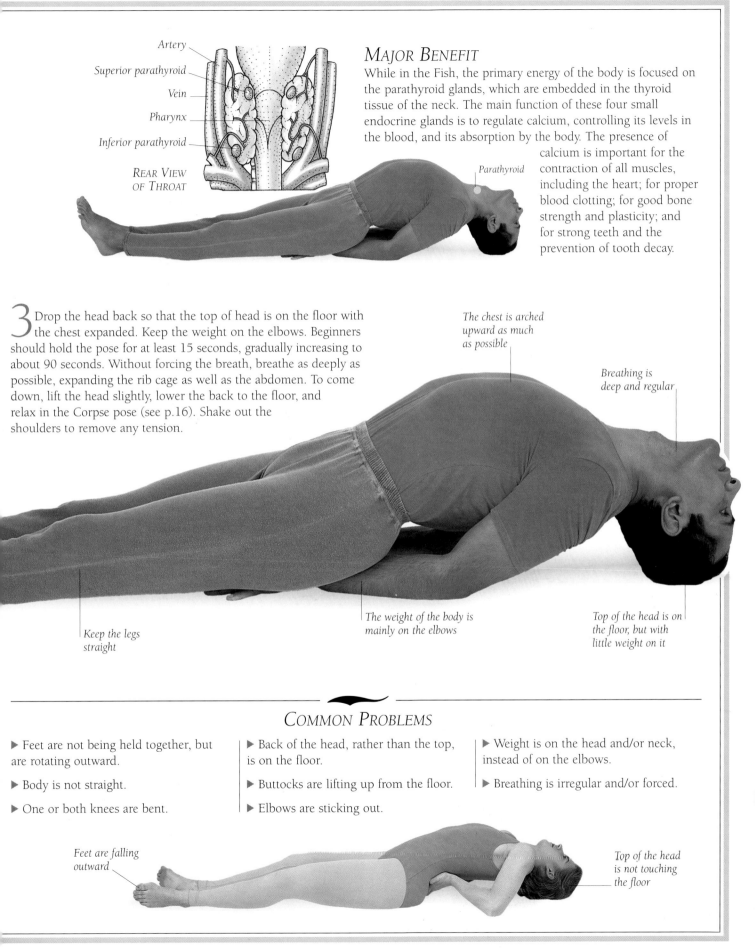

Artery
Superior parathyroid
Vein
Pharynx
Inferior parathyroid

REAR VIEW
OF THROAT

Parathyroid

MAJOR BENEFIT

While in the Fish, the primary energy of the body is focused on the parathyroid glands, which are embedded in the thyroid tissue of the neck. The main function of these four small endocrine glands is to regulate calcium, controlling its levels in the blood, and its absorption by the body. The presence of calcium is important for the contraction of all muscles, including the heart; for proper blood clotting; for good bone strength and plasticity; and for strong teeth and the prevention of tooth decay.

3 Drop the head back so that the top of head is on the floor with the chest expanded. Keep the weight on the elbows. Beginners should hold the pose for at least 15 seconds, gradually increasing to about 90 seconds. Without forcing the breath, breathe as deeply as possible, expanding the rib cage as well as the abdomen. To come down, lift the head slightly, lower the back to the floor, and relax in the Corpse pose (see p.16). Shake out the shoulders to remove any tension.

The chest is arched
upward as much
as possible

Breathing is
deep and regular

Keep the legs
straight

The weight of the body is
mainly on the elbows

Top of the head is on
the floor, but with
little weight on it

COMMON PROBLEMS

▶ Feet are not being held together, but are rotating outward.

▶ Body is not straight.

▶ One or both knees are bent.

▶ Back of the head, rather than the top, is on the floor.

▶ Buttocks are lifting up from the floor.

▶ Elbows are sticking out.

▶ Weight is on the head and/or neck, instead of on the elbows.

▶ Breathing is irregular and/or forced.

Feet are falling
outward

Top of the head
is not touching
the floor

FISH *Variations*

Once you have mastered the Fish pose and can hold it for at least
2 minutes, you may want to try one of these advanced variations.

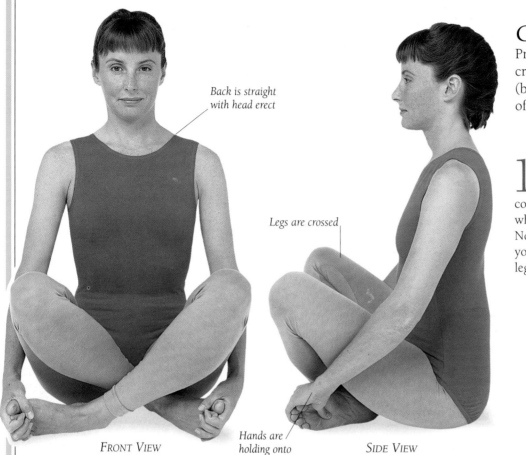

*Back is straight
with head erect*

Legs are crossed

FRONT VIEW

*Hands are
holding onto
the feet*

SIDE VIEW

CROSS-LEGGED

Practicing the Fish with the legs
crossed, or in the Lotus position
(bottom left), helps to prevent loss
of prana through the lower limbs.

1 ◁ Start by sitting in the Easy Sitting
position (see p.17). You should feel
comfortable in this pose before trying
what is an advanced Fish variation.
Now lift your knees slightly, and bring
your arms around the outside of the
legs. Hold onto your feet firmly.

*Both knees must
be on the floor*

FISH IN LOTUS POSITION

This is an advanced variation. It is better not
to attempt it until you can sit comfortably in
a good "tight" Lotus (see p.63) with
the feet high up on the
opposite thighs and
knees close together.

*Chest is arching upward with
rib cage fully expanded*

*Both knees are
on the floor*

Hands are holding feet

Elbows are on the floor

*Top of the head
is resting on
the floor*

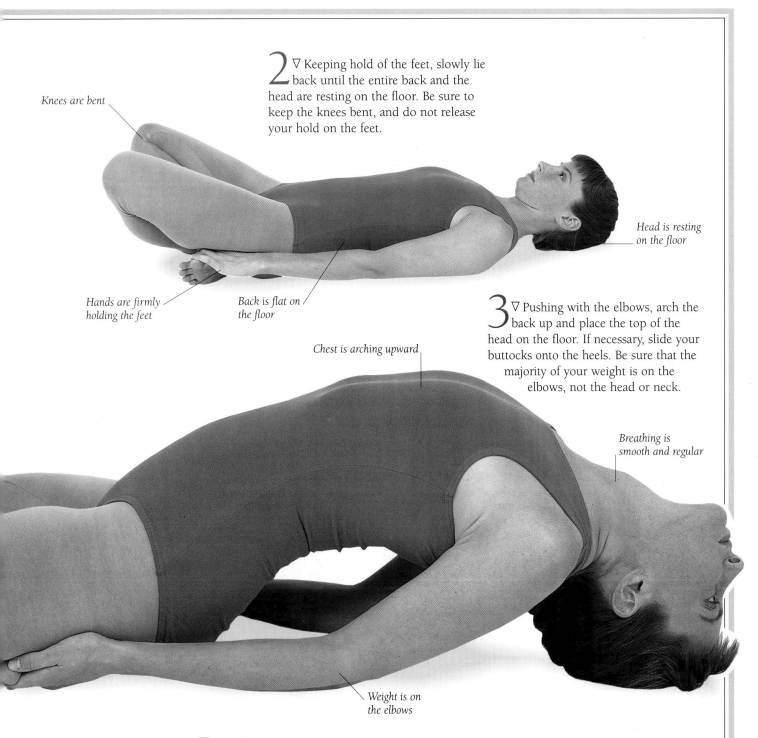

2 ▽ Keeping hold of the feet, slowly lie back until the entire back and the head are resting on the floor. Be sure to keep the knees bent, and do not release your hold on the feet.

Knees are bent

Head is resting on the floor

Hands are firmly holding the feet

Back is flat on the floor

Chest is arching upward

3 ▽ Pushing with the elbows, arch the back up and place the top of the head on the floor. If necessary, slide your buttocks onto the heels. Be sure that the majority of your weight is on the elbows, not the head or neck.

Breathing is smooth and regular

Weight is on the elbows

COMMON PROBLEMS

▶ One or both knees are raised up from the floor.

▶ Body is twisted to one side.

▶ Head is not touching the floor.

▶ Neck is twisted to one side.

▶ Weight is on the head or neck, instead of on the elbows.

▶ Chest is not arching upward.

▶ Breathing is irregular, or fast, or breath is being held.

▶ The back of the head, instead of the top of it, is resting on the floor.

Knee is lifting from the floor

5

THE FORWARD BEND

Paschimothanasana

In this asana, the body is folded almost in half, giving a comprehensive stretch to the entire back of the body, from the skull down to the heels. It is a very simple yet powerful position to practice. In the words of the *Hatha Yoga Pradipika*, "This most excellent of asanas makes the breath flow through the Sushumna, rouses the gastric fire, makes the loins lean, and removes all diseases." (For Forward Bend variations, see pp.56–9.)

ॐ PHYSICAL BENEFITS

▶ Powerfully massages all the abdominal organs.
▶ Stimulates and tones the digestive organs, increases peristalsis, and relieves constipation and other problems.
▶ Counteracts obesity and enlargement of the spleen and liver.
▶ Regulates the pancreatic function, providing a valuable aid for those with diabetes or hypoglycemia.
▶ Mobilizes the joints and increases elasticity in the lumbar spine.
▶ Relieves compression of the spine and sciatica.
▶ Strengthens and stretches the hamstrings.

ॐ MENTAL BENEFITS

▶ Greatly enhances concentration and mental endurance.
▶ Invigorates the mind and nervous system, controlling many nervous complaints.

ॐ PRANIC BENEFITS

▶ Balances the prana; meditation is possible only when the vital energy is centered.
▶ Establishes perennial "youth."

1 To come into Paschimothanasana, sit with the head, neck, and back in a straight line. The legs are together in front of the body with the knees flat on the floor.

Legs are stretched out with the knees straight

Toes are back toward the head

Arms are parallel, next to the ears, with the elbows straight

Spine is elongated and the entire back is stretching upward

2 Inhale as you stretch both arms over the head, stretching them up alongside the ears. Elongate the spine; feel as though you are making yourself as tall as possible.

Toes are back toward the head

52

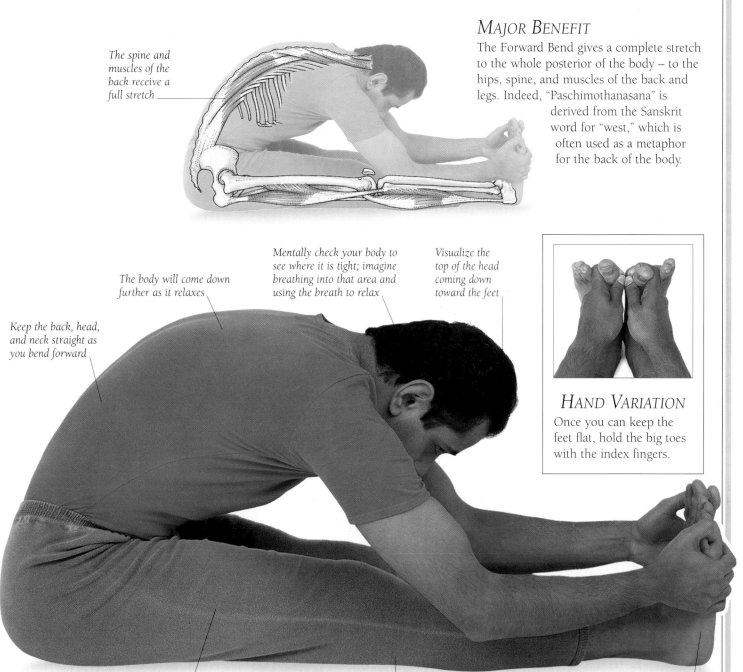

The spine and muscles of the back receive a full stretch

MAJOR BENEFIT

The Forward Bend gives a complete stretch to the whole posterior of the body – to the hips, spine, and muscles of the back and legs. Indeed, "Paschimothanasana" is derived from the Sanskrit word for "west," which is often used as a metaphor for the back of the body.

The body will come down further as it relaxes

Mentally check your body to see where it is tight; imagine breathing into that area and using the breath to relax

Visualize the top of the head coming down toward the feet

Keep the back, head, and neck straight as you bend forward

HAND VARIATION
Once you can keep the feet flat, hold the big toes with the index fingers.

Do not allow the feet, legs, or hips to rotate outward

Legs are straight with the backs of the knees on the floor

Feet are together and flat with the toes back toward the head

3 △ Exhale, and bend forward from the hips. Reach forward to grab hold of the feet as you bring the chest down toward the thighs. If you cannot reach the toes, grasp the ankles or even the shins. Hold the position for at least 10 seconds, gradually increasing to about 3 minutes. Repeat 3–5 times. To release the position, inhale, and stretch your arms and body up (see Step 2).

COMMON PROBLEMS

▶ Knees are bent upward.

▶ Back is rounded and the head, rather than the chest, is down toward the knees.

▶ The feet are apart and the toes are rotating outward.

▶ Toes are not pointed back.

Bring the chest, not the head, toward the legs

THE INCLINED PLANE

As a counterpose, the Inclined Plane complements the complete stretch given to the back of the body in the Forward Bend position. When practiced on a regular basis, the Inclined Plane strengthens the shoulders, arms, and hips, and increases their flexibility, as well as developing balance and muscular coordination.

1 To come into the Inclined Plane, begin by sitting up with both legs straight out in front of you. Place the hands flat on the floor behind your back with the fingers pointing backward. Drop your head back and rest on your hands.

Head is back

Take a few deep breaths in preparation

Feet and legs are together, and straight out in front of the body

Hands are flat on the floor with fingers pointing backward

Hips are up as high as possible

Head is back

Keep the feet together and flat on floor

2 Inhale as you lift the hips as high as possible, trying to bring the feet flat on the floor. Try to hold the pose for at least 10 seconds, gradually increasing to 1 minute. Breathe normally as you hold the position. Lower the hips to the floor, and gently shake out the hands to relax.

Fingers are pointing backward

COMMON PROBLEMS

▶ Head is allowed to come forward, rather than dropping back.

▶ There is tension in the neck and shoulders.

▶ Hips are rotated outward and/or dropped. They should be raised as high as possible.

▶ One or both of the knees are bent.

▶ Hands are rotated outward.

▶ Feet are not flat on the floor.

▶ Feet are not straight, but are falling out to the sides.

▶ Legs are apart.

Body does not form a straight line

INCLINED PLANE Variations

When you can hold the Inclined Plane comfortably for at least 30 seconds, you may want to try some variations. These positions require considerable strength and concentration.

Lift one leg as high as possible

Head stays back

One arm is straight up, with the fingers pointing toward the ceiling

Do not allow the hips to drop

Keep the hips up

Try to keep the knee straight

ONE LEG UP △

From the Inclined Plane, keep the head back, and inhale as you lift one leg toward the ceiling. Hold it up for a few seconds, lower it to the floor, and repeat with the other leg.

Knees are straight

ONE ARM UP △

The second variation is slightly more tricky and requires considerable concentration. Keeping both knees straight and your shoulders as parallel to the floor as possible, inhale and lift one arm toward the ceiling. Hold it straight up for a few seconds, then lower it and try to raise the other arm.

Hold the ankle or toes of the opposite leg

Stretch the leg up toward the face

Both knees should remain straight

OPPOSITE SIDES

When you have mastered both of the above variations, you are ready to try this one, which combines the two. With your hips up, inhale as you raise one arm and the opposite leg. Hold onto the ankle or foot, and bring it as close to the face as possible. Hold for a few seconds. Lower the arm and leg, and repeat with the other arm and leg.

Foot is flat on the floor

Hips are as high as possible

FORWARD BEND
Variations with Knees Bent

Many people suffer from lower back pain as a result of time spent hunched in front of a computer screen, desk, or steering wheel. These habits cause the back to become tight and greatly weakened. Janu Sirasana, a variation of the Forward Bend, stretches and strengthens both the lumbar and the thoracic regions.

PREPARATORY EXERCISE

◁ Sit with the left leg straight out in front of you. Bend the right knee and place the sole of the right foot flat against the inner left thigh. Using your right hand, gently bounce the right knee toward the floor for about 1 minute.

Left leg is stretched out in front of the body

Gently bounce the right knee with the right hand

Face straight ahead with your back erect

Do not allow the body to twist

1 Stretch both arms straight up above the head as you inhale. With the arms straight alongside the ears, feel that you are stretching as high as possible.

Make sure that the weight is evenly distributed on both buttocks

Left leg is stretched out straight in front

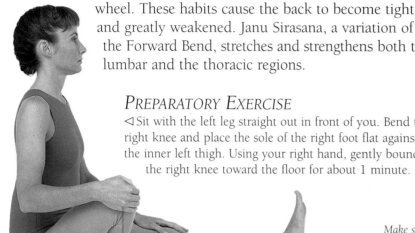

2 Exhale as you reach forward, bending from the hips, to hold onto the left foot. Keep the body straight. Hold for 10 seconds, gradually increasing to 1 minute. Inhale as you stretch upward. Repeat the exercise on the other side.

Stretch the head forward

Holding the right foot with both hands, stretch the toes back toward the head

Bring the chest as close to the thigh as possible

Elbows are evenly spaced on either side of the leg

HALF LOTUS FORWARD BEND

If you are very flexible, try the above asana in the "bound" Half Lotus. With your left foot high on your right thigh, bring your left arm behind the back and grab hold of your left foot. Bend forward and hold onto the right foot with the right hand. Hold for as long as is comfortable. Release the foot, and inhale as you sit up. Repeat on the other side.

Shoulders are equidistant from the floor

Head is forward, and the back is straight

Use the breath to relax into this position

THE BUTTERFLY

From a sitting position, bend both knees, and bring the soles of the feet together. Grasp the feet with both hands, and draw them in as close to the body as possible, keeping the back straight. Gently bounce the knees to help relieve tension in the lumbar and hip regions. You should be able to hear a soft thump each time the knees touch the floor. Continue this bouncing movement for 1–3 minutes before proceeding to the variations below.

Keep the head erect

Keep the back straight to gain maximum relaxation of the muscles in the lumbar region

Hold the feet in toward the body

Gently bounce the knee down to the floor and up again

Soles of the feet are flat against each other

BHADRASANA

With the knees wide apart (see above), use the elbows to push the knees and thighs gently toward the floor. Exhale as you lower the chest toward the feet. Hold for about 10 seconds, but once you can relax and breathe into the position, try to increase the time to 1 minute.

CHEST TO FEET

This further variation has a stronger stretching effect on the inner thighs and hips. Turn the feet until the soles face up toward the body, and bring the chest down to the feet.

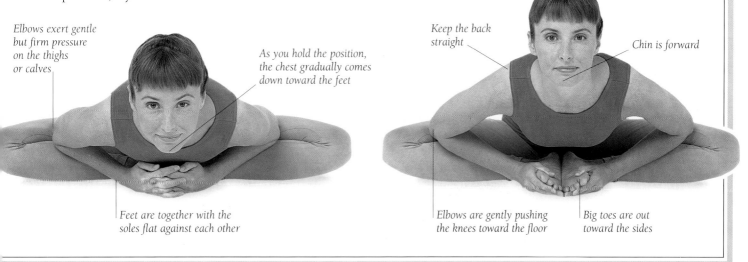

Elbows exert gentle but firm pressure on the thighs or calves

As you hold the position, the chest gradually comes down toward the feet

Keep the back straight

Chin is forward

Feet are together with the soles flat against each other

Elbows are gently pushing the knees toward the floor

Big toes are out toward the sides

FORWARD BEND
Variations with Legs Apart

This is a series of increasingly difficult exercises. Their purpose is to make the spinal column more flexible, to limber up the lumbar region, strengthen the neck muscles, massage the thyroid gland, and increase the chest capacity. These variations also help to speed up digestive functions.

STARTING POSITION

This is the initial position for all the other postures on this page. Bring your legs as wide apart as you can. Stretch both arms up over the head as you inhale deeply. You can now proceed to practise the following asanas, remembering to come back to this position between exercises.

Both arms are stretched up alongside the ears, in preparation for the succeeding asanas

Keep the elbows straight

Head, neck, and spine are in a straight line and are stretched upward

Legs are as wide apart as possible

Toes are pointed back toward the body

VARIATION 1 ▽

Turn to your left, and exhale as you come straight down onto the left leg. Keep the opposite buttock firmly on the floor. If the body is not properly aligned, you will not get the full benefit from the pose. Hold for 10–30 seconds, breathing deeply. Inhale as you stretch up. Repeat on the right.

Shoulders should be parallel to each other and to the floor

Both hands reach forward to grip the left foot and stretch it back toward the head

Chest and chin are on the thigh

Keep this leg flat on the floor

Try to bend the elbows onto the floor on either side of the leg

VARIATION 2 ▽

From the starting position, twist the body to face right. Exhale as you come down toward the left leg. Both hands grasp the left foot. The left elbow rests on the floor inside the left knee. Look up, and hold for 10–30 seconds. Inhale, and repeat on the opposite side.

To stretch further, imagine that you are trying to get the spine onto the thigh

Breathe while you hold the pose

Top shoulder is back as far as possible

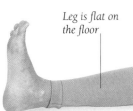

Leg is flat on the floor

Both buttocks are firmly on the floor

Bottom shoulder comes forward

VARIATION 3 ▽

Exhale as you bring the body forward. Grasp the toes of both feet. Breathe slowly and deeply. Try to bring the forehead to the floor. If you can, try to bring the chin, and finally the chest, to the floor.

Don't allow the body to bounce up and down

Keep the back straight to get the maximum stretch in the lumbar region

Hold the feet with the respective hands

Use the breath to sink more deeply into the position

TORTOISE - *KURMASANA* ▽

This pose stretches the spinal column and rejuvenates the whole nervous system. From the starting position, bend the knees upward slightly. Place the hands, with palms downward and fingers pointing back, on the floor. Slide the arms beneath the knees. Slowly straighten the knees, bringing the chest toward the floor.

Tension is released from the shoulder region, making this an excellent exercise for those who work on computers

Arms are beneath the legs, with the hands and fingers pointing backward

Chin is stretched forward on the floor, bringing blood to the throat region and massaging the thyroid

THE SHOOTING BOW

Akarna Dhanurasan, or the Shooting Bow, stretches the legs, hips, and lumbar region, strengthens the hands and feet, and invigorates the nerve impulses to these regions. Regular practice of this asana has been found to help in alleviating rheumatism in the limbs, and it can even relieve sciatica.

STARTING POSITION

Sit up with the legs stretched straight out in front of you. Reach forward to grab hold of the toes of both feet. This is the starting position for the following asanas. Be sure to return to it after each pose, before proceeding to the next position.

Sit up with the head and chest as straight as possible

Right hand holds right foot; left foot is in left hand

Back is straight

HAND POSITION
Bring the index fingers between the first two toes of each foot, and grip the big toes.

Feet are together with heels stretching forward, toes back toward the head

TRADITIONAL SHOOTING BOW

This is the classical pose, in which one foot is drawn back toward the ear as an archer would draw a bow. Without letting go of either foot, bend the right knee. Inhale as you pull back and up with the right elbow, bringing the right foot as close to the right ear as possible. Breathe as you hold the position. Repeat on the other side.

Bring the foot up to the ear, rather than dropping the head to the foot

Keep the chest and head up

Keep a firm hold on the toes of the opposite foot

SHOOTING BOW
Variations

By moving the limbs in slightly different directions, these variations on the Shooting Bow bring additional benefits.

VARIATION 1

Keeping the weight firmly on both buttocks, inhale as you raise the right leg. Visualize yourself bringing the straight leg up alongside the ear, without relinquishing your grip on the opposite foot. Hold the position for at least 2–5 deep breaths. Practice 2–3 times on each leg.

Look straight ahead

Raised leg is straight

Lower leg is kept straight

Keep a firm hold of the opposite foot

VARIATION 2

Bend the left knee and place it on top of the right thigh. Hold the left foot with the right hand. Extend the left hand to hold the right foot. Bending the right elbow, inhale and pull back, bringing the left foot up toward the right ear. Hold for 3–5 seconds before lowering. Repeat on the opposite side.

Right elbow is pulled back behind the right ear

Chest is lifting up

Left elbow is straight

Index finger is hooked around the big toe

Right leg is straight

EKA PADA SIRASANA

This One Foot to Head pose is an advanced position, providing a full stretch for both the lumbar and thoracic regions. Be sure to warm the body up properly before attempting it. You should never force or strain to come into any position.

1 From the Easy Sitting position (see p.17), lift the right leg and place the right foot into the bend of the left elbow. Bring the right arm outside leg and clasp the hands. Gently rock to and fro for a few minutes.

Head is erect

Leg is held up high

Both arms are outside the right leg, "hugging" it close to the chest

Back is straight

2 ▷ Release the right leg. Take hold of the right foot with both hands and gently try to bring the sole of the foot flat against the breastbone. Slowly slide the foot toward the chin, then the nose, and finally up to the forehead.

Knee points outward and back

3 ▽ Release the hold on the foot. Drop the right shoulder down slightly for a moment, bringing it under the right knee, and then straighten the body as much as possible.

Keep the head up

Leg is back and over the shoulder

Try to sit upright, to avoid compressing the back and chest

4 ◁ Slowly straighten the knee, bringing the foot behind the head. Try to bring the hands into the Prayer pose at the chest. Hold the position for a few seconds. Repeat this series of exercises with the left leg.

Hands are together at the chest, palms flat against each other

LOTUS

This classic sitting pose, also known
as Padmasana, is greatly revered as
a position for meditation and
pranayama because
it enhances
concentration.

*The entire body now
resembles a three-
dimensional triangle
with a secure base*

*Keep the body erect with
the head, neck, and chest
in a straight line*

*Right knee
should
remain on
the floor*

*Place the right foot as
high on the left thigh as
you find comfortable*

1 △ From the Easy Sitting position (see p.17),
take hold of your right foot with both hands
and place it on your left thigh. The foot will turn
slightly so that the sole is facing upward.

2 Next, take hold of the left foot and bring
it up onto the right thigh. For meditation,
place the hands in Chin Mudra pose or join
them in other positions (see p.17).

*Make sure that both knees
are firmly on the floor*

COMMON PROBLEMS

▶ Knee(s) are lifted off the floor.

▶ Back is rounded, or twisted to one side.

▶ Foot is not high enough on the thigh.

▶ Body is leaning to one side.

▶ The back is hunched, compressing the
rib cage and impeding proper breathing.

▶ Shoulders are hunched and not level.

▶ Head is drooping, or twisted to one side.

▶ Shoulder blades are too far apart.

▶ Upper body is leaning forward, instead
of being perpendicular to the floor.

▶ CAUTION: Many people, particularly
Westerners, find the Lotus position a
difficult one to achieve. Beginners are not
recommended to try it.

*Head is
drooping
forward*

*Shoulders
are hunched*

6

THE COBRA

Bhujangasana

The *Gerunda Samhita* notes that this asana, which resembles a cobra with its hood raised, "increases the bodily heat, destroys diseases, and by the practice of this posture the Serpent-Goddess (Kundalini) awakens."

PHYSICAL BENEFITS

▶ Increases flexibility, rejuvenates spinal nerves, and brings a rich blood supply to the spinal region.
▶ Works, massages, and tones the back muscles.
▶ Stretches the thoracic region and expands the rib cage, bringing relief from asthma.
▶ Massages all organs through gentle pressure on the abdomen.
▶ Helps relieve problems of the uterus and ovaries, and menstrual problems.

MENTAL BENEFITS

▶ Demands considerable concentration, and thus strengthens this faculty.

PRANIC BENEFITS

▶ Stimulates pranic flow to the lung, stomach, kidney, bladder, and spleen meridians.
▶ Awakens the Kundalini (potential spiritual energy), thus assisting the realization of one's full potential.
▶ Bhujangasana produces body heat.

STARTING POSITION ▽

This is the relaxation position before and after each of the next few asanas. As you relax on your abdomen, breathe as deeply as you did on your back in the Corpse pose.

Head is turned to one side, resting on the hands

Legs are relaxed, with the toes pointing inward and the heels out to the sides

Feel the abdomen press against the floor as you inhale, and rise as you exhale

1 ▽ Bring the legs together and the forehead to the floor. Place the hands, palms downward, on the ground directly beneath the shoulders. Visualize the slow, graceful movement of the snake as you prepare to roll the body upward.

The elbows are bent, slightly raised, and tucked in toward the sides

Keep the legs together

Fingers point forward, tips in line with the top of the shoulders

2 Begin with the head bent downward and the forehead touching the floor.

3 As you inhale, slowly raise the forehead and bring the nose to the floor.

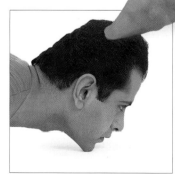

4 Roll the head upward, raising the nose and brushing the chin on the floor.

MAJOR BENEFIT

The Cobra is always practiced as the first in a series of backward bending movements. Its effect is to arch the spine back gently, promoting flexibility of the lower back in particular. The gentle pressure that the pose brings to bear on the abdomen also has a beneficial massaging effect on the internal organs.

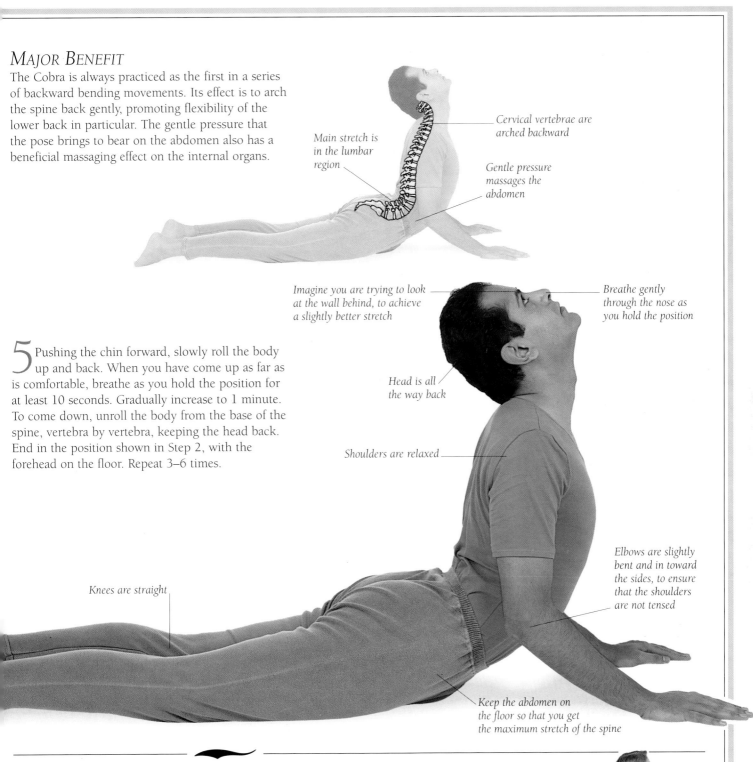

Main stretch is in the lumbar region

Cervical vertebrae are arched backward

Gentle pressure massages the abdomen

5 Pushing the chin forward, slowly roll the body up and back. When you have come up as far as is comfortable, breathe as you hold the position for at least 10 seconds. Gradually increase to 1 minute. To come down, unroll the body from the base of the spine, vertebra by vertebra, keeping the head back. End in the position shown in Step 2, with the forehead on the floor. Repeat 3–6 times.

Imagine you are trying to look at the wall behind, to achieve a slightly better stretch

Breathe gently through the nose as you hold the position

Head is all the way back

Shoulders are relaxed

Knees are straight

Elbows are slightly bent and in toward the sides, to ensure that the shoulders are not tensed

Keep the abdomen on the floor so that you get the maximum stretch of the spine

COMMON PROBLEMS

▶ Using the arms to push the body up into the Cobra, rather than rolling the body up into the position.

▶ Elbows are straightened and the shoulders are tensed and hunched.

▶ One arm is pushing harder than the other, causing the body to twist.

▶ Abdomen is lifted off the floor.

▶ Head is dropping forward.

▶ CAUTION: Do not practice the Cobra while pregnant, although this asana is an excellent way to prepare the body for pregnancy.

Never tense the shoulders

COBRA Variations

Once you have mastered the Cobra, it is recommended that you attempt some of the variations, to achieve the maximum backward stretch for the spine, improving its flexibility. These Cobra variations will also further strengthen the back muscles, as well as increasing the lung capacity.

Head is back

HANDS RAISED IN FRONT

From Step 1 of the Cobra, lift the hands 2in (5cm) from the floor. Roll up into the Cobra without using the arms. This will help to strengthen the back muscles. Hold it for at least 10 seconds, gradually increasing to 30 seconds.

Body is arching up as much as possible

Keep the feet and legs on the floor

Hands are up off the floor with the palms facing downward

HANDS BEHIND BACK

From Step 1 of the Cobra, clasp the hands behind the back. With the elbows straight, push the palms toward the feet as you roll up. Raise the hands toward the ceiling. Hold for 10 seconds or more.

Raise the arms as high as possible to increase shoulder and upper back flexibility

Stretch the head back

Fingers are interlocked and palms face the feet

Keep the head back and the back up

OVER THE SHOULDER COBRA

The Cobra itself is the starting position for this and for the King Cobra poses. Turn and look over the right shoulder; try to see the left heel. Hold this position for a few seconds, and then repeat on the other side. Return to the center before rolling down or attempting other variations.

Shoulders are relaxed and back

Elbows are slightly bent

Hips are on the floor

As you become more proficient, try to keep the heels together

KING COBRA

From the Cobra, move the legs apart and walk the hands back toward the hips as far as possible. Most people will have to straighten their elbows a bit, and perhaps come up onto the fingertips. Now bend the knees and bring the feet up to the head.

Chest expands as the shoulders are arched back

Allow the abdomen to rise slightly from the floor

Keep the hips and buttocks down

KING COBRA - KNEE HOLD

This last variation requires a great deal of strength, flexibility, and concentration. From the King Cobra, lift the hands up from the floor one at a time. Reach the hands back and take hold of the respective knees.

Head is back as far as possible, with the feet resting on the top

Breathe as deeply as possible

Hands have a firm hold on the knees, pulling them in toward the body

Arch the chest forward

THE LOCUST

Salabhasana

The Locust gives a wonderful backward bend to the spine, serving as a counterpose to the Shoulderstand, the Plow, and the Forward Bend. You should master the Half Locust (Steps 1–2) before attempting the Full Locust (Step 3).

PHYSICAL BENEFITS
▶ Brings a rich blood supply to the spine.
▶ Tones the nerves and muscles, particularly in the neck and shoulders.
▶ Increases abdominal pressure, regulating intestinal function and strengthening the abdominal walls.
▶ Improves sluggish digestion.
▶ Expands the chest, benefiting sufferers from asthma and other respiratory problems.
▶ Strengthens shoulder, arm, and back muscles.
▶ Regular practice of the Locust relieves back pains and sciatica.

MENTAL BENEFITS
▶ Encourages concentration and perseverance.

PRANIC BENEFITS
▶ Stimulates pranic flow in the lung, stomach, spleen, heart, liver, small intestine, pericardium, and bladder meridians.
▶ "Increases the digestive fire" – an ancient Yogic way of saying that the energy flow maximizes the use of all nutrients.
▶ Produces body heat.

1 Lie face down on the floor with the legs straight out behind you, and the hands side by side under the thighs.

Tops of the feet are flat on the floor

Knees are straight

Hands are beneath the thighs, with the insides of the wrists touching

Imagine that you are trying to get the throat flat on the floor

Both legs are straight

2 For the Half Locust, inhale as you raise the left leg. Do not twist the hips or bend the knee. Retain the breath as you hold for at least 5 seconds. Exhale as you lower the leg, and repeat on the other side. Raise the legs alternately 2–5 times each.

Tune the raising and lowering of the leg to the breath

Chin is stretched forward

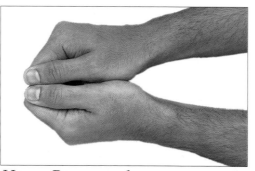

HAND POSITION 1
Making fists of the hands, bring them together beneath the thighs with the wrists touching.

HAND POSITION 2
If you find this position more comfortable, clasp the hands together and interlock the fingers.

MAJOR BENEFIT

The Locust brings flexibility to the cervical (upper back) region and strength to the lower back, but it is important to stretch the chin as far forward as possible if these benefits are to be gained. When you first attempt the Locust, you may be disappointed to find that your feet rise only slightly from the floor. Do not be discouraged. This will improve rapidly with practice.

Lower back is strengthened

Flexibility of the upper back is improved

3 When you are comfortable with the Half Locust, progress to the Full Locust. From Step 1, take 3 deep breaths. On the last, raise both legs as high as possible. Breathe, and hold for at least 5 seconds, gradually increasing to 30 seconds. Come down, and repeat 2–5 times. When you have finished, relax on your abdomen.

Legs are straight and lifting as high as possible

Hands are together

Elbows are straight, and as close together as possible

Chin is stretched forward on the floor

COMMON PROBLEMS

▶ Jumping, or trying to throw, the legs into the position.

▶ The nose or forehead, rather than the chin, is resting on the floor.

▶ The chin is lifted off the floor.

▶ Hips are twisted.

▶ Knees are bent.

▶ One leg is higher than the other.

▶ Hands are twisted into different positions.

▶ Hands are apart instead of being held together.

▶ Breath is being held while in the position.

▶ CAUTION: The Locust should not be attempted while pregnant, since it puts pressure on the abdomen.

The legs should never be jumped up into the Locust position

LOCUST *Variations*

Once you have mastered the Locust, your back is ready to try the following variations. For these, you may find it helpful to place the hands palms downward on the floor. In the Full Locust, with the feet raised directly above the head, the body is in exactly the opposite position to that of the Shoulderstand (see pp.34–7). The first two variations should not be attempted until you are able to lift your legs to an angle of 45 degrees above the floor in the Locust.

STARTING POSITION

Legs are together and knees straight

HIGH LEGS ▷

From the Full Locust, push the hands against the floor to gain extra leverage, inhale, and lift the legs up directly over the head. This position promotes strength and flexibility in the back and shoulder muscles.

Bend the knees and bring the feet down to the head

Entire spine is bent backward

Feet are resting on the top of the head

Lift the hips as high as possible

FEET TO HEAD △

Once you can hold the legs over the head (see High Legs), you are ready for the next step. Bend the knees and, without too much strain, hold the position and breathe as deeply as possible. The weight of the feet and legs will gradually bring the feet to the head.

Head is back, with the chin stretched as far forward as possible

Keep the hands and elbows together

The body is resting on the chin

LOCUST IN LOTUS

This variation on the Locust is an advanced asana that promotes great flexibility in the hip, lumbar, and cervical, regions of the back.

1 Begin in the Lotus position (see p.63). Only advanced students, who are able to hold the Lotus comfortably for a long time, should attempt this variation.

2 From the Lotus, bring your hands to the floor in front of you and stand up on the knees. Gradually walk the hands forward, allowing the body to follow.

Hips are stretching in the opposite direction as the body comes forward

Back is straight and the head is erect

Right foot is on the left thigh

Left foot is on the right thigh

Both knees are on the floor

Use the hands to walk the body forward

Try to bring the hips down to the floor

3 ◁ Come over onto the abdomen. Bring the hips down as flat on the floor as possible. Stretch the chin forward. Clasp the fists and bring the hands beneath the body.

Hands are under the thighs, with the elbows as close together as possible

4 ▽ Inhale and lift the knees as high as possible. Breathe deeply as you hold the position for as long as you feel comfortable. You can repeat the asana 3–4 times. Then come out of the Lotus and relax on your abdomen.

Lift the legs as high as possible

Push the hands onto the floor

8

THE BOW

Dhanurasana

The Bow gives a full backward bend to all parts of the back, combining and enhancing the benefits of the Cobra and the Locust. These three exercises form a set and should be practiced together. As the Forward Bend flexes the spine, the Bow extends it.

PHYSICAL BENEFITS

▶ Massages and invigorates the internal organs, especially the digestive organs.
▶ Strengthens the abdominal muscles.
▶ Expands the chest region – a benefit to people suffering from asthma and other respiratory problems.
▶ Enhances the elasticity of the spine.
▶ Massages all the muscles of the back.
▶ Just as the Forward Bend hyperextends the spine, so the Bow hypercontracts it.

MENTAL BENEFITS

▶ Regular practice develops internal balance and harmony.
▶ Strengthens concentration and mental determination.

PRANIC BENEFITS

▶ The person who practices the Bow regularly can never be lazy, but will be full of energy, vigor, and youthful vitality.
▶ Stimulates the lung, small intestine, stomach, liver, and urinary bladder meridians.

Knees are bent, with the feet close to the buttocks

Clasp hold of the ankles, not the tops of the feet; the feet are relaxed

Bring the forehead to the floor

1 △ Lying on your abdomen, place the forehead on the floor. Bend the knees, bringing the feet up. Reach back to grasp the respective ankles. The feet should be relaxed. There is no need to point the toes, as this uses energy unnecessarily.

2 ▷ Keeping the arms straight, inhale as you arch the entire body upward. Lift the head, chest, and thighs off the floor. Hold the position for at least 10 seconds, increasing gradually to 1 minute. Repeat the pose 3–5 times.

ROCKING BOW

With the head back and the body arched upward, use the breath to rock the body back and forth. Inhale as you rock back, and exhale as the body comes forward. Remember to keep the elbows straight.

Rock forward while exhaling

Rock backward while inhaling

MAJOR BENEFIT

The Bow gives a full backward bend to the whole of the spine and all the muscles of the back, from the neck to the lower back, or lumbar region.

Entire body is bent backward

Keep your head back and look up; this will lift the chest higher

Keep the elbows straight

Bring the feet as high, and as far away from the body, as possible

The entire body is resting on the abdomen

COMMON PROBLEMS

▶ Hands are clasped around the feet, rather than around the ankles.

▶ Only the upper part of body is being lifted up from the floor.

▶ Elbows are bent, and the knees are bent too sharply, allowing the heels to come down to the buttocks.

▶ Body is twisted to one side.

▶ Head is forward, rather than being stretched up and back.

▶ CAUTION: Do not attempt the Bow or any Bow variation while pregnant, as these asanas increase the pressure on the abdomen.

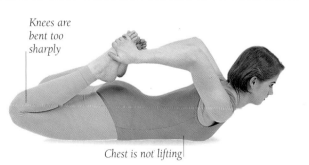

Knees are bent too sharply

Chest is not lifting

BOW *Variations*

As the spine and shoulders gain flexibility, you can begin to attempt the following advanced variations of the Bow. The first sequence shows the steps for moving from the Bow into the Full Bow position, an asana that produces an even more comprehensive bending of the spine.

1 Rest on the abdomen with the knees bent and the feet raised. Lift the head and the chest from the floor. Turn the toes outward slightly, and bring the hands under and around the feet. Take hold of the feet and grasp them firmly.

Lift the head and chest

2 Gradually rotate the shoulders, bending the elbows and bringing them down, then out and forward in front of the face. As the elbows come forward, the knees and thighs lift from the floor.

Hold the feet firmly as the elbows rotate down, out, and then forward

PREPARATORY EXERCISE - HALF FULL BOW

1 If you are unable to come into the Full Bow, this variation will encourage the necessary flexibility. With the elbow bent, bring the hand under the foot to grip it.

2 Swivel the elbow down, out, and forward.

3 Practice with one arm and the same leg, holding for at least 30 seconds, before releasing and repeating the exercise on the other side.

4 Repeat on the other side. One arm is resting on the floor to support the body. The other is grasping the foot. Concentrate on gripping the foot firmly. The elbow is brought alongside the face and points forward.

Push the body up, using the bottom arm

3 Arch further to come into the Full Bow. Breathe, and hold the pose for as long as is comfortable. Once you can hold it for 30 seconds or more, you can try to rock backward and forward, without releasing your grip on the feet.

The elbows are forward and up

Head is back

The chest is fully expanded

Thighs are raised as far as possible

FEET TO HEAD
From the Full Bow, gently try to bring the feet down and place them on the top of the head.

Feet are on top of the head

FEET TO SHOULDERS
This even more advanced variation, bringing the feet to the shoulders, requires great flexibility of the entire spine and shoulders.

Back is very strongly arched

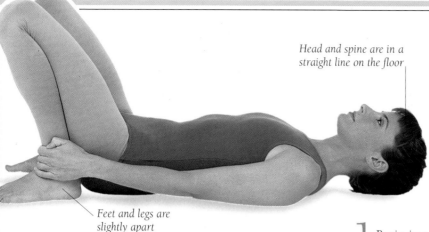

Head and spine are in a straight line on the floor

Feet and legs are slightly apart

Feel the stretch in the chest and upper back area, as well as in the hips

Feet are flat on the floor

Back of the head and the shoulders remain on the floor

The body is prepared to arch higher

Elbows are bent with the arms on either side of the head

THE WHEEL
Chakrasana

This asana strengthens the muscles of the abdomen and thighs. It makes the back and hips supple, improves memory, and is said to relieve afflictions of the trachea and larynx.

1 Begin in a preliminary pose, lying flat on your back with your knees bent. Place both feet flat on the floor close to the buttocks. Reach down and grasp the respective ankles with both hands.

2 Keeping the feet, head, and shoulders on the floor, arch the hips and chest up as high as possible. Breathe deeply and gently as you hold for at least 10 seconds. Lower the hips to the floor for a few moments and repeat 3–5 times.

3 When you find that Step 2 has become easy (which may take several weeks of practice), you can try this next step. With the hips up as high as possible, release the grip on the ankles and bring the hands to the floor behind the shoulders.

Palms are flat on the floor with the fingers pointing in toward the shoulders

4 With the feet and knees parallel, begin to lift the body off the floor by pushing with the hands and feet. As the body begins to rise, the hips will lead, followed by the chest. The neck will arch back as you bring the top of the head to the floor in preparation for the final Wheel position.

Hips are stretching upward

More flexible people
may try to straighten
the knees

Head is down
between the arms

5 Inhale as you straighten the elbows,
arching the hips and chest up as high as
possible. Allow the head to drop back. Breathe
deeply as you hold this position for at least
10 seconds, gradually increasing. When you
find that you can hold it comfortably for
30 seconds, you may want to try some of the
variations shown on the following pages.

Keep the
elbows
straight

Do not allow the feet to turn
outward, as this will rotate the
hips as well, and you will lose
the correct alignment of the body

COMMON PROBLEMS

▶ Hips are dropped, instead of
pushing upward.

▶ Head is resting on the floor.

▶ Feet and knees are turned out.

▶ Legs are not extended.

▶ Hips are rotated outward,
spoiling the alignment of the body.

▶ Feet are not flat on the floor.

▶ There is no comprehensive arch
to the back.

▶ Body is twisted to one side.

▶ Hands are not in line with each
other on either side of the head.

▶ Arms are not extended.

Shoulders are
not arched
upward

STARTING POSITION

WHEEL *Variations*

When you feel that you can stand firmly and comfortably in the Wheel, many variations await you. These are designed to bring an even greater increase of strength and flexibility to the spine, shoulders, and upper back.

ONE LIMB RAISE

From the Wheel, inhale, and raise one leg. Hold for a few seconds. Lower, and repeat using the other leg. Then lift each arm. When you have mastered raising each limb, try the next pose.

Heel stretches upward

Hips are lifting upward

Elbows are straight

SAME SIDE RAISE

Raise one leg as high as possible, and then raise the arm on the same side. Place the hand on the thigh. Hold for up to 30 seconds. Repeat 2–3 times on each side.

Lift the leg as high as possible before bringing the hand to rest on the thigh

Do not allow one hip to lift higher than the other, tipping the body to one side

STANDING WHEEL

Advanced students can try to come into the Wheel from a standing position. This will give you a complete backward bend to all parts of the back, neck, shoulders, and limbs. Relax at the end of Step 1 before proceeding to Steps 2 and 3.

2 ▽ Bring the arms up and back, and continue to arch the body backward. Look at the floor behind your head, and imagine placing your hands on it.

3 ▽ Slowly lower the hands to the floor, bending the knees more as necessary. Hold for as long as you feel comfortable, breathing deeply. Repeat the pose several times if you wish.

Hang the head back

Hips are arched forward

1 ◁ With the feet parallel and shoulder width apart, arch backward slightly. Hang the arms down and relax the hands on the backs of the legs.

Knees are slightly flexed

Arms are straight and alongside the head

Arch the entire back

Hands are ready to be placed on the floor

Stretch the hips upward

Hands are flat and parallel

HANDS TO FEET

From the Wheel, walk the hands in toward the feet. Take very small steps with the hands. Imagine that you are trying to catch hold of the heels. If you practice on a regular basis, you will find yourself rapidly gaining flexibility in the spine and shoulder joints.

Elbows are straight

Feet and knees are parallel and pointing straight ahead

ELBOWS TO GROUND

From the Hands to Feet pose, take hold of the heels, bend the elbows, and bring them down onto the floor. Inhaling, lift one leg up and bring it back toward the chest. Hold for as long as you feel comfortable. Lower the leg, and repeat with the other leg. Practice 2–3 times on each side, then drop the hips and relax.

Knee is straight

Leg is stretching back

Hips are arched up as high as possible

Knees and feet remain pointing ahead

Head is reaching toward the feet

Hold the heel firmly with both hands

79

BACKWARD BENDS

Here we have a series of backward bending asanas that begin in Vajrasana, sitting on the heels with knees and feet together and the whole weight of the body on the knees and ankles. Each of these backward bends brings great steadiness to the body, as well as giving an excellent backward bend to the spine and back muscles. Vajrasana resembles Namaz, the Muslim prayer pose, and is a traditional Zen pose for meditation.

STARTING POSITION: VAJRASANA

Sit up on the heels with the feet, knees, and legs together. This is Vajrasana, which stimulates digestion. Try sitting like this while eating, or after a meal.

Back is straight

Hands rest on the thighs

THE CAMEL

This position, known as the Asana of Firmness or the Sitting Wheel, strengthens the thighs while improving the flexibility of the back.

1 ▷ From Vajrasana, inhale as you lift the hips and trunk, standing up on the knees to prepare for the Camel. The hips and body rise, but the legs and feet do not change position.

Head and body are facing straightforward

Arms are resting by the sides

Legs and feet may be together or parallel

2 ▽ With the right hand, clasp hold of the right heel. If you find it difficult to reach the heel, place the right hand flat on the floor behind the right foot.

Stretch back with one arm first

Do not allow the knees to slide apart

3 ▽ Allowing the head to drop back, reach down with the left hand to grasp the left heel (or place the left hand flat on the floor parallel to the right hand). Breathing gently, hold for at least 10 seconds, gradually increasing to 1 minute. Sit back on the heels and relax in the Child's pose (see p.26). Repeat 2–3 times.

Chest is lifting upward

Head is dropping back

Back, arms, and legs form a rectangle

Hips and thighs are stretching forward

FULL DIAMOND -
POORNA SUPTA VAJRASANA

Full Diamond in Vajrasana is an
advanced and challenging asana.

1 From Vajrasana, lie back onto the
heels. Imagine that you are trying
to bring the back flat onto the floor,
though the heels are under the body.
Keep the heels parallel to each other
beneath the body.

*Neck, head, and
shoulders are all
on the floor*

*Heels are beneath
the body with the
legs parallel*

*Back is as flat and close
to the floor as possible*

*Chest and neck are
arching upward*

2 ▷ Place the hands flat on the floor behind
the shoulders, as you did when preparing
to come into the Wheel (see pp.76–7).
Lift the chest, sliding the top of the
head onto the floor.

*Hips and chest are
arching upward*

3 ◁ Pushing with the hands, lift the hips and chest as
high as possible. Gradually "walk" the hands and head
toward the feet. Do not be discouraged if the hands and
feet do not meet; with practice, your backward bending
will improve. Hold for 10 seconds, gradually increasing to
1 minute. Relax in the Child's pose (see p.26) before
continuing with your asanas.

*Head and neck are
dropped back*

*Top of the head is on the
floor and/or as close to the
feet as possible*

*Forearms
are resting on
the floor*

*Both hands hold the foot firmly: if you
cannot reach with the left arm, catch hold
of the right wrist with the left hand*

PIGEON - KAPOTHASANA

From Vajrasana, straighten the right knee and slide
the leg back until the right thigh is by the left foot.
Bend the right knee until the foot and calf are
upright. Reach both arms over the head and
catch hold of the right foot. Drop the head back
and try to bring the right foot to the top of the
head. Hold for at least 10 seconds. Return to
Vajrasana, and repeat on the other side.

*Chest is "puffed"
forward, like a
pigeon*

*Back and neck are
arched back, giving
the upper body a
full backward bend*

THE CRESCENT MOON
and Variations

An excellent backward-bending exercise, the Crescent Moon also stretches the hips, thighs, and legs. It is a beautiful flowing series of positions that promotes balance and concentration. When you practice it properly, you will derive great inner peace. All the Crescent Moon variations should be performed on both sides.

Eyes look straight ahead, as though at the horizon

Front knee is bent, with shin upright

Palms are flat against each other at the center of the chest

1 From Vajrasana (see p.80), rise up on the knees. Bring the right foot flat onto the floor in front of the body.

Chest is lifting upward and body is erect

Foot is elongated, with the toes stretched backward

Shin and top of the foot are flat on the floor

2 ▷ Bring the palms together at the chest in Prayer position. Hold this pose for a few moments to achieve your physical and mental balance, in preparation for the Crescent Moon.

Feel the thigh lifting upward

HANDS TO ANKLE

When you have sufficient spinal flexibility, continue from Crescent Moon, arching back until you have caught hold of your back foot. Even if you cannot reach the foot, imagine this in your mind.

Head is stretched back, trying to see the foot

Front foot is firmly on the floor

Thigh is almost parallel to the floor, feeling as though it is lifting upward

Back foot is flat on the floor; you may find it more comfortable to tuck the toes under, for greater balance

Back is as straight as possible

ANJANEYASANA

From Step 1 above, lift the toes of the front foot and slide the heel forward, until the back of the front leg and the front of the back leg rest on the floor. Keep facing forward. Bring the hands to the chest in Prayer pose.

Keep the chest up, and try not to lean forward

Keep the legs straight; do not allow the hips to twist

Arms are stretched back

3 Straighten the elbows, stretching the arms up and back over the head. As the arms arch back, allow the body to follow. Be aware of keeping the palms flat against each other and the arms straight alongside the ears. Hold for as long as it feels comfortable. Repeat on the other side.

Chest and the entire upper body are arched

Head is dropped back

Knee is directly above the toes

Hips are lifting and stretching forward

Top of the foot remains flat on the floor

Keep the right foot flat on the floor

CRESCENT ANJANEYASANA

From Anjaneyasana, straighten the elbows. Keeping the palms flat against each other, bring the arms up and alongside the ears. Arch back into this variation of the Crescent Moon that benefits the spine, hips, and thighs.

Elbows are pointing upward on either side of the head

Head is back to the foot

PIGEON IN ANJANEYASANA

From Anjaneyasana, bend the back knee and bring the foot up toward the head. Bring both arms over the head, catch hold of the foot, and try to bring it to the head.

Chest is arched and facing straight ahead

Head is back with arms alongside the ears

Be careful to keep the hips straight

Legs should be straight, and flat on the floor

Hips must be straight, not rotated to either side

Front heel is stretching forward

THE SPINAL TWIST

Ardha Matsyendrasana

After the forward and backward bending of the spine, the Spinal Twist gives a lateral stretch to the vertebrae, back muscles, and hips. This important asana takes its Sanskrit name from the great sage Matsyendra, one of the first teachers of Hatha Yoga.

PHYSICAL BENEFITS

▶ Helps to keep the spine elastic by retaining side-to-side mobility.
▶ Helps to relieve muscular problems in the back and hips.
▶ Removes adhesions in the joints caused by rheumatism.
▶ Increases the synovial fluid of the joints, and makes the joints active.
▶ Tones the roots of the spinal nerves and the sympathetic nervous system, and brings a fresh supply of blood to the area.
▶ Massages the abdominal muscles, relieving digestive problems.
▶ Benefits the gall bladder, spleen, kidneys, liver, and bowels.

MENTAL BENEFITS

▶ Helps to cure disorders of the nervous system.
▶ Brings peace of mind.

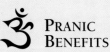

PRANIC BENEFITS

▶ Augments the prana sakti (vigor and vitality), removing innumerable diseases.
▶ Rouses the Kundalini (potential spiritual energy).

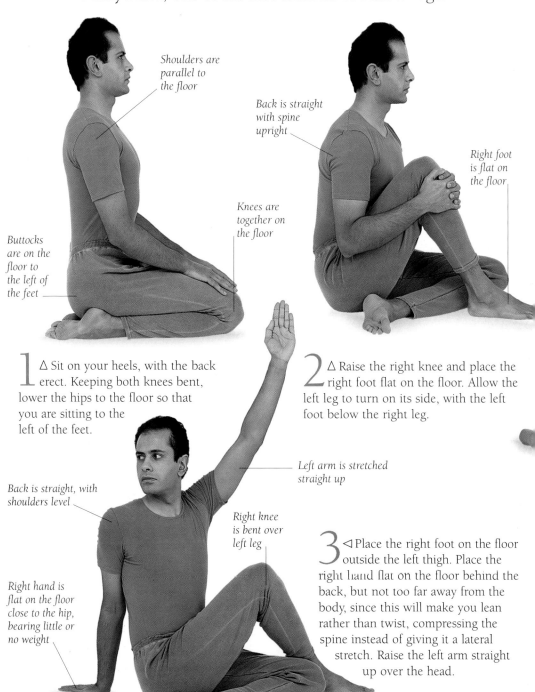

Shoulders are parallel to the floor

Buttocks are on the floor to the left of the feet

1 △ Sit on your heels, with the back erect. Keeping both knees bent, lower the hips to the floor so that you are sitting to the left of the feet.

Back is straight with spine upright

Right foot is flat on the floor

Knees are together on the floor

2 △ Raise the right knee and place the right foot flat on the floor. Allow the left leg to turn on its side, with the left foot below the right leg.

Left arm is stretched straight up

Back is straight, with shoulders level

Right hand is flat on the floor close to the hip, bearing little or no weight

Right knee is bent over left leg

3 ◁ Place the right foot on the floor outside the left thigh. Place the right hand flat on the floor behind the back, but not too far away from the body, since this will make you lean rather than twist, compressing the spine instead of giving it a lateral stretch. Raise the left arm straight up over the head.

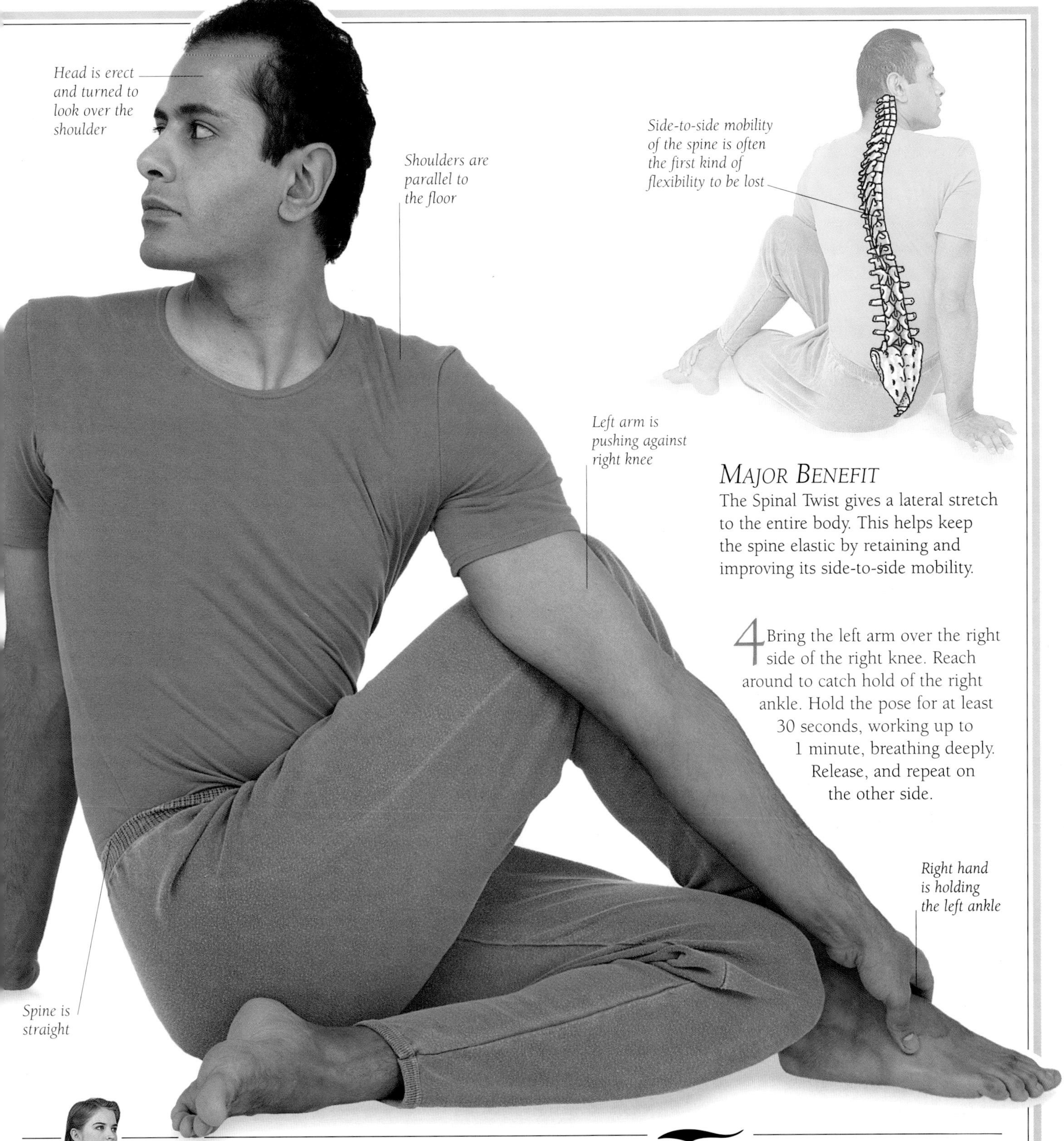

Head is erect
and turned to
look over the
shoulder

Shoulders are
parallel to
the floor

Side-to-side mobility
of the spine is often
the first kind of
flexibility to be lost

Left arm is
pushing against
right knee

MAJOR BENEFIT
The Spinal Twist gives a lateral stretch
to the entire body. This helps keep
the spine elastic by retaining and
improving its side-to-side mobility.

4 Bring the left arm over the right
side of the right knee. Reach
around to catch hold of the right
ankle. Hold the pose for at least
30 seconds, working up to
1 minute, breathing deeply.
Release, and repeat on
the other side.

Right hand
is holding
the left ankle

Spine is
straight

If the body leans, rather
than twisting, you will
not gain the benefit
of the asana

COMMON PROBLEMS

▶ Buttocks are lifting off the floor.

▶ Back is not straight, and the body is
leaning, rather than twisting laterally.

▶ Looking over the wrong shoulder.

▶ Hand is allowed to hang freely, rather
than clasping the opposite ankle.

▶ Foot is not flat on the floor.

▶ Back hand is too far from the body.

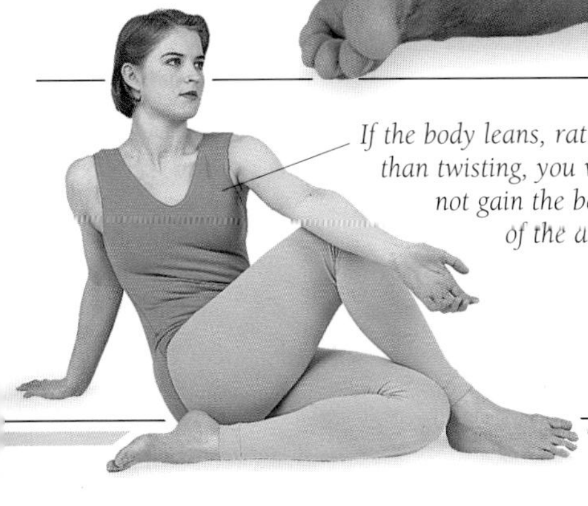

STARTING POSITION

SPINAL TWIST
Variations

"Matsyendrasana increases appetite by fanning the gastric fire, and destroys terrible diseases in the body.... It rouses Kundalini and makes the moon steady." – *Hatha Yoga Pradipika*

Head is rotated so that you are looking over the right shoulder

WRIST GRASP

This is a variation of the Spinal Twist. From the basic position (see p.85), release the hold on the ankle. Without dropping the shoulder, bring the left hand under the right knee, and reach behind the back to grasp the right wrist. Hold this pose for as long as you would hold the basic position. Release your grasp, bring the body to the center, and repeat in the opposite direction.

It is essential to keep the back straight and the shoulders level

Left foot is flat on the floor; do not allow the toes to lift, or the foot to rotate outward

As you become more supple, try gradually bringing the foot closer to the hip

BEGINNERS' VARIATION

If you are unable to do the basic Spinal Twist (see pp.84–5), try this simple variation with one leg straight. Sit with both legs straight out in front of the you. Bend the right leg, bring it over the left, and place the foot flat on the floor just outside the left knee. With the right hand flat on the floor behind the body, raise the left arm, bring it over the right knee, and grasp the right ankle. Keep the back as straight as possible.

Head is turned to look over the right shoulder

Shoulders are parallel to the floor

Left arm is pushing against the right knee

Left hand is grasping the right ankle

Right hand is flat on the floor

Left leg is stretched out straight

ANKLE CLASP ▷

This is an advanced asana that may take you many months to perfect. When you are able to bring the foot close to the hip, release the hold of the left hand on the right wrist; catch hold of the right ankle with the right hand. The left arm is in front of the right knee, holding the left knee. Hold for as long as possible. Release, and repeat on the other side.

Left arm is around the right knee, grasping the left knee

Right foot is flat on the floor, next to the left hip

Shoulders are level, and the chest is fully expanded

Right arm is behind the back, holding the right ankle

Right arm crosses behind the back to hold the right foot

Left arm crosses in front of the chest to hold the left foot

Both legs are bent at the knee with one leg crossed over

Feet are next to the opposite hips

FULL SPINAL TWIST ▽

From a sitting position, place the right foot at the top of the left thigh, and the left foot outside the right knee. Reach behind the back and take hold of the right foot with the left hand. Grasp the left foot with the right hand, and turn your head as far to the left as you can. Hold for as long as possible, breathing gently. Return the body to the center, and repeat on the other side.

Right hand is holding the left ankle, with the elbow pushing against the knee

Left arm reaches round to the right thigh

Chest is expanded and upright

KNEES TOGETHER △

Bend both knees, with the right knee directly over the left knee. Bring the right arm behind the back, and grasp the right foot. The left arm crosses the body to hold the left foot. Hold for 10 seconds, gradually increasing to 1 minute. Release, and repeat on the opposite side.

Right foot rests on the left thigh, in Half Lotus position

10A

THE CROW

Kakasana

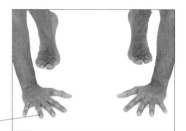

The Crow and the Peacock (see pp.90–1)
are excellent balancing exercises that promote
physical and mental balance. You should
perform one or the other as a basic asana.

Head is erect

1 ◁ To prepare for the Crow, come into a squatting position with the feet flat on the floor and the arms between the knees.

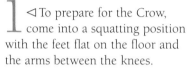

Fingers are spread wide apart and turned slightly inward

2 △ Place the palms flat on the floor directly below the shoulders. Spread the fingers like the feet of a crow.

Feet and knees are wide apart

3 ▷ Bend the elbows outward, so that the upper arms can act as supports. Rise onto your toes, and rest the knees on the respective upper arms.

Hands are directly beneath the shoulders

Head is lifted up

Weight is on the toes

Weight is on the wrists, with the toes being used for balance

4 ◁ Focus the eyes on a point a little way in front of the body, and inhale deeply. Retain the breath as you gradually shift the weight forward onto the hands. You will feel the stretch in the forearm and wrist. This is an excellent position for combating the ravages of tendonitis.

MAJOR BENEFIT

Since the Crow demands a high level of
concentration, it enhances this faculty. The
position also brings a flow of energy to
the lower arms, wrists, and hands.

Hips are raised

*Nerves and
muscles of the
forearms are
invigorated*

*Keep the head up,
or the weight will
shift and you will
find yourself
rolling forward*

*Feet are up
but relaxed*

*Knees are resting
on the upper arms*

5 Shifting the balance entirely onto the
hands, slowly lift the feet off the floor. If
this proves difficult, try raising one foot and
then the other. Breathe deeply as you hold the
position for as long as you feel comfortable. If
you cannot lift the feet, keep practicing Step 4
until the arms and wrists are strong enough.
(For Crow variations, see pp.92–3.)

*The entire weight of the body
is now balanced on the hands*

COMMON PROBLEMS

▶ Head is dropped forward.

▶ Hands are in the wrong position.

▶ Weight is on one side, rather than
being balanced.

▶ Concentration is lacking.

▶ Fingers are together, instead of being
spread wide apart.

*Body is not
balanced*

10B

THE PEACOCK

Mayurasana

The peacock, with its long tail feathers, symbolizes beauty and immortality in Indian tradition. This pose is an alternative to the Crow (see pp.88–9).

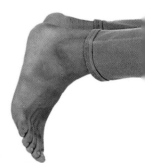

1 ◁ Kneel down; sit back on your heels with the knees wide apart. Lift the arms up in front of the body, and bring the elbows, forearms, and hands together, with the palms facing upward.

Knees are out to the sides

Heels are together; buttocks are resting on the heels

2 ▽ Place the palms of both hands on the floor, with the fingers pointing backward. Bend forward, and place the abdomen on the elbows.

Elbows are bent, pressing up into the abdominal region

Hands are flat on the floor between the knees, with the fingers pointing in toward the body

Try to keep the elbows together

3 ▷ Slowly lean forward, and lower your head until the forehead is resting on the floor. If the pressure on the wrists seems too great, continue to practice for a few days, or even weeks, before proceeding to Step 4.

PHYSICAL BENEFITS

▶ Combats all types of digestive problems.
▶ Massages all parts of the digestive system through pressure of the elbows, revitalizing the liver and digestive organs.
▶ Relieves such problems as indigestion, diabetes, constipation, and hemorrhoids.
▶ Strengthens arm and wrist muscles and develops flexibility, relieving repetitive strain injuries.
▶ Develops physical balance and alignment.

MENTAL BENEFITS

▶ Enhances mental balance, concentration, and determination.
▶ Removes lethargy and general feelings of weakness and helplessness.
▶ Eases many mental disorders.

PRANIC BENEFITS

▶ The position of the elbows stimulates and enhances pranic flow to the spleen, kidney, heart, lung, small intestine, and pericardium meridians.
▶ Awakens Kundalini shakti (full psychic potential).

4△ First stretch one leg straight back, and then bring the other leg out beside it. This position brings great flexibility and strength to the wrists and forearms.

Legs are fully extended

The body is resting on the toes, hands, and head

MAJOR BENEFIT

The principal benefit of the Peacock asana derives from the pressure that the placement of the elbows puts upon the abdomen. This massages and revitalizes the internal organs, curing many digestive diseases.

Pressure from the elbows massages the internal organs

5▽ Lift the head off the floor. The body is now resting on the hands and toes. Take a deep breath and gradually begin to shift the weight of the body forward.

Weight is on the toes and the hands

Hands are pointing toward the feet

6▽ Do not attempt to lift the feet. Let them rise as the weight shifts forward. Hold for at least 10 seconds, breathing gently. Gradually increase to 1 minute. Repeat 2–3 times before resting.

The legs, trunk, and head are in a straight line parallel to the floor

The body is balanced on the hands

As you breathe, you will experience the benefit of the elbows pressing into the abdomen

Head is held up

Leg is being thrown up into the position

Elbows are apart

COMMON PROBLEMS

▶ Trying to jump, or throw the legs, up into the position.

▶ Elbows are not together.

▶ Weight may shift to one side, causing you to topple over sideways.

▶ Hands are not centered, but are out toward the sides.

▶ Concentration is lacking.

▶ CAUTION: This position should not be attempted while pregnant.

CROW *Variations*

Although all asanas are designed as mental as well as physical exercises to prepare the mind and body for meditation, it is the balancing poses that give the most noticeable improvement in the powers of concentration.

Both elbows are straight

Both knees are to the left of the arms

Palms are flat on the floor with the fingers spread widely

SIDE CROW - *PARSWA KAKASANA*

To come into the Side Crow, begin in a squatting position with both knees to the left of the body.

1 ◁ Place the hands on the floor beneath the shoulders, and slide the right hand forward about 2in (5cm). This will make it easier to balance.

2 ▷ Focus the eyes on a point about 1½ft (50cm) in front of the body. Gently shift your weight forward onto the left arm and raise both feet off the floor. Hold for as long as possible, breathing deeply. Repeat 3–6 times, and then try it on the other side.

Keep the head up

Arms are fully extended and lifting the body off the floor

Legs are together with knees bent, resting on the left arm

Head must remain up, with the eyes focused on a fixed point in front of the body

Knees are straight

Body is as parallel to the floor as possible

Keep the right hand slightly in front of the left

CURVED POSE - *VAKRASANA*

Once you can hold the Side Crow comfortably, begin to straighten the knees, bringing the feet straight out to the side. This position requires greater physical strength and concentration. Be sure to practice on both sides.

FEET TO SIDES

Assume the Crow pose (see pp.88–9) with the knees resting on either arm. Slowly straighten each leg from the knee. Hold this position for as long as you feel comfortable.

Inner thigh is resting on the arm

Both feet are extended out in front on either side of the body

Hands are directly beneath the shoulders

Shoulder and wrist muscles are greatly strengthened

COCK POSE - *KUKUTASANA* ▷

This advanced asana, which starts in the Lotus pose (see p.63), requires a great deal of hip flexibility. Slide each arm into the space between calf and thigh. Place the hands flat on the floor and, shifting the weight forward, stand up on the hands.

Arms bear the full weight of the body

Each foot is resting on the opposite thigh

PEACOCK
Variations

Once you can hold the Peacock pose easily (see pp.90–91), try these variations. If you can do the Lotus, you may find the Peacock in Lotus easier than the regular Peacock.

The back and legs are in a straight line

HEELS UP

From the Peacock, slowly lower the chin to the floor holding the body straight, raising the legs at an angle to the floor. Hold for as long as you feel comfortable.

The chin is down toward the floor, with the feet extended up in the air

The body's center of balance is different because the legs do not extend out as far

PEACOCK IN LOTUS

Begin in the Lotus position (see p.63). Using your hands, stand up on your knees, lean forward, and, placing the elbows against the midriff, follow the steps for coming into the Peacock. Your center of balance will have changed, facilitating the position.

Knees are raised as high as possible

Entire weight of the body is on the hands

Elbows are pressing into the midriff

93

THE TREE

The asanas shown here are further balancing exercises. For the most part, these are physically simple, and yet they are mentally highly demanding. These postures develop, to the highest degree, the powers of mental concentration and single-mindedness of thought, as well as physical balance.

1 ▽ Stand up straight, balancing on the right foot. Bend the left knee and, helping with your hand, place the foot against the opposite thigh with the knee pointing outward.

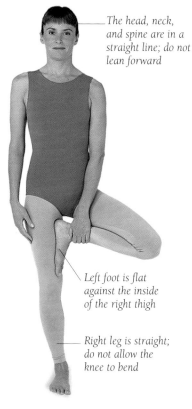

The head, neck, and spine are in a straight line; do not lean forward

Left foot is flat against the inside of the right thigh

Right leg is straight; do not allow the knee to bend

2 ▽ Focus on a point straight in front of you. Release your hold on the foot and bring both hands together at the chest in Prayer position. Find your balance.

Palms are flat against each other at the chest

The body is balanced on the right leg; try not to waver

Keep the eyes focused on a point in front of you

Arms are alongside the ears, and the elbows are straight

Breathing is very slow and gentle

3 Keeping the palms together, slowly extend the arms above the head. Hold for 30 seconds, breathing gently, gradually increasing to 3 minutes. You will experience an exhilarating sensation of lightness, as though the prana is virtually lifting you off the floor. Release, and repeat on the other side.

COMMON PROBLEMS

▶ Body is leaning to one side, or twisted with one hip pushing out.

▶ Standing knee is bent or rotated outward.

▶ Palms are not flat against each other.

▶ Elbows are not straight above the head.

▶ Thumbs are crossed, instead of side by side.

▶ Bent knee is coming forward, rather than pointing out to the side.

▶ Eyes are looking downward.

▶ Mind lacks proper concentration.

ADVANCED BALANCES

These poses are for more advanced and more flexible students. Focusing the eyes on a point in front of you is the key to balancing the body.

HALF LOTUS TREE ▷

For this Tree variation, place the foot on the opposite thigh in Half Lotus position. Hold the pose for as long as you feel comfortable. Make sure you practice on both sides.

Left foot is on top of the left thigh, in Half Lotus pose

Breathing is very gentle and relaxed

Right leg, spine, neck, head, and both arms are all in a straight line

EAGLE - GARUDASANA ▽

Stand erect, balanced on your right leg. Bring the left leg across and in front of the right, and hook the foot behind the right ankle. With the right arm upright in front of the face, bring the left arm across and in front of your right, then behind it. Try to have the palms as flat together as possible. Repeat on the left leg.

Shoulder flexibility is greatly enhanced

Spine and head are in a straight line; do not lean forward

Balance and concentration of mind and body are strengthened

Palms are together above the head or at the chest

Eyes are fixed on a point straight in front of you

Spine, head, and neck are in a straight line

Great flexibility is brought to the hips and lower limbs

TIP-TOE POSE - PADANDGUSHTASANA ▷

Kneel with the buttocks on the heels. Place the left foot on the right thigh in Half Lotus. Place your hands on the floor next to you and slowly shift the weight forward onto the toes of the right foot. Bring the hands together at the chest. Hold for as long as you feel comfortable. Repeat on the opposite side.

Back and neck are straight

◁ VATYANASANA

Standing up straight, place the left foot on the right thigh in Half Lotus. Slowly bend the right knee until the left knee rests on the floor. Hold for as long as possible. Stand up and repeat on the other side.

Buttocks rest on the heel of the right foot

NATARAJASANA

Nataraja, Siva as the Cosmic Dancer, destroys and re-creates the universe with each step. He symbolizes the constant flow of energy and matter, and the destruction of the old self in preparation for the creation of the new. This asana stretches the upper body and develops balance.

1 ▷ Stand with the body facing straight ahead. Bend the right knee, lifting the foot until it is close to the buttock. Grasp the ankle with the right hand. Hold the position for a moment until you feel balanced and ready to proceed to Step 2.

Right hand has a firm grasp on the right ankle

Body is balanced on the left leg

2 ▷ Inhale as you stretch the left arm up. With the elbow straight, bring the arm alongside the left ear. Keep the eyes focused on a point in front of you to maintain balance.

Breath is slow and relaxed

Left leg, spine, neck, head, and left arm are in a straight line

3 ▷ Without releasing the hold on the ankle, slowly begin to shift the line of the body, breathing normally. Stretch the right foot away from the buttock. Straighten and lift the right knee until the right thigh is parallel to the floor.

Chin is parallel to the floor

Keep the weight firmly on the left foot; do not waver from side to side

FULL NATARAJASANA

As well as developing balance, this advanced pose provides a full backward bend to the upper body.

Left hand joins the right

Right arm is bent and reaching back to grasp the toes of the right foot

Head is back, giving a full backward bend to the spine and neck

Arms are parallel on either side of the face

1 From Step 3 above, slide the hand from the ankle up to the toes, rotating the shoulder in the way described for the Full Bow (see p.74, Step 2). Hold, and repeat on the other side.

2 Arching the head back, try to bring the foot to the head. Hold for as long as is comfortable. Release the hold, lower the foot, and repeat on the other side.

Body is firmly balanced on one leg; make sure it is kept straight

4 Focus the eyes on a point on the floor just in front of the body. Keep the left arm alongside the ear, and slowly shift the weight forward until the chest and arm are parallel to the floor. Hold the position for as long as you feel comfortable. Release, and practice on the other side.

Keep the foot up as high as possible

Keep the arm straight and alongside the ear

Right arm is pulling against the right leg

Remember to breathe as you hold the position

The right thigh, spine, neck, head, and left arm are in a straight line, parallel to the floor

Foot is planted firmly on the floor

COMMON PROBLEMS

▶ Bent knee is not lifting.

▶ Body is turning outward.

▶ Standing leg is bent.

▶ Upper body is upright, rather than leaning forward.

▶ Right arm is not parallel to the right thigh.

▶ Arm is not alongside the ear.

▶ Head is twisted to one side.

▶ Upper foot, rather than the ankle, is being held.

▶ Standing foot is not firmly planted; this allows the body to waver.

▶ Eyes are not focused on a point in front of the body.

▶ Breathing is erratic or tense.

▶ Mind is not concentrating, making it difficult to maintain balance.

Body is not leaning forward

Hand is grasping the foot

11

THE STANDING FORWARD BEND

Pada Hasthasana

This is the first of the standing poses. In effect it is similar to Paschimothanasana, the sitting Forward Bend (see pp.52–3). If it is remembered that "you are as young as your spine," Pada Hasthasana will be seen as a veritable elixir of youth. Its practice promotes a continued youthful vigor throughout life.

ॐ PHYSICAL BENEFITS

▶ Lengthens the spine, making it supple and elastic. Can even give a little extra "growth."
▶ Mobilizes the joints.
▶ Invigorates the entire nervous system.
▶ Stretches the hamstrings and muscles of the back of the legs and the lower body.
▶ Stretches all the muscles on the posterior side of the body.
▶ Rectifies shortening of the legs resulting from fractures, and can correct inequalities in the length of the legs.
▶ Increases the blood supply to the brain.

ॐ MENTAL BENEFITS

▶ Greatly enhances concentration.
▶ Expels tamas (inertia or laziness), stimulating intellectual capacities.

ॐ PRANIC BENEFITS

▶ Renders the body light by expelling tamas.
▶ Purifies and strengthens the Sushumna nadi (the central astral nerve tube that induces meditation).
▶ Invigorates the Apana Vayu (downward-moving, or efferent, prana).

1 With the legs together, center the weight of the body on the balls of the feet. Inhale deeply as you stretch both arms straight up over the head. Feel as though the entire body is extending upward.

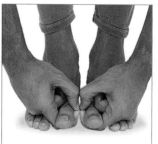

Body is straight, with the arms up alongside the ears

Legs are together

HAND VARIATIONS

Once you have gained sufficient flexibility in the back of the legs, and are able to hold the Standing Forward Bend comfortably for several minutes, you may wish to try these three hand position variations. They stretch the muscles in different ways.

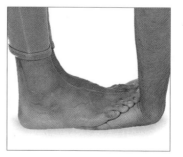

VARIATION 1
Reach behind the legs and catch hold of each elbow with the opposite hand.

VARIATION 2
Lift the front of the feet off the floor, slide the hands under them, and lower the feet.

VARIATION 3
For this traditional hand position, bring the forefingers around the respective big toes.

2 Exhale, stretching down toward the floor. grab hold of the back of the legs wherever you feel comfortable. Breathe gently as you hold this position for at least 10 seconds. Gradually increase the time to 1 minute. As you hold the pose, feel the hips stretching upward.

Keep the body weight centered; do not allow the hips to drop backward

Knees are straight

Hold the legs wherever you can comfortably reach, without straining or bending the knees

Forehead is in toward the legs

Feet remain next to each other

MAJOR BENEFIT

The Standing Forward Bend gives a complete stretch to the entire posterior of the body, from the back of the scalp to the back of the heels. The position enables the body to take advantage of the force of gravity. If the head and neck are kept relaxed, their weight will aid the body in stretching a bit farther, provided that the knees are not allowed to bend.

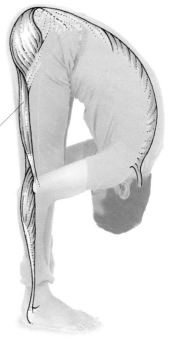

All the muscles of the back of the body are stretched

COMMON PROBLEMS

▶ Weight of the body is on the heels.

▶ Back is rounded.

▶ Weight is unevenly placed, causing the body to tilt to one side.

▶ Feet are apart and/or turned out.

▶ Knees are bent.

▶ Hips are dropping back.

▶ Head is forced toward the knees.

Legs should be straight

Feet are apart and not parallel

12

THE TRIANGLE

Trikonasana

The last of the 12 basic asanas, the Triangle provides the entire body with an invigorating lateral stretch. When practiced on a regular basis, it makes the body feel lighter and improves all other asanas.

ॐ PHYSICAL BENEFITS

▶ Stretches the spine and trunk muscles.
▶ Tones the spinal nerves and abdominal organs, improving the working of the bowels.
▶ Practice of the Triangle improves the appetite and assists digestion.
▶ Promotes flexibility of the hips, spine, and legs.
▶ Reduces or eliminates pain in the lower back.
▶ Invigorates the circulation.
▶ Practice is especially beneficial to anyone who suffers from a shortening of one leg as a result of a fracture of the hip, thigh bone, or bones of the lower leg.

ॐ MENTAL BENEFITS

▶ Alleviates anxiety and hypochondria.
▶ Reduces mental stress.

ॐ PRANIC BENEFITS

▶ Stimulates pranic flow to the spleen, liver, large intestine, gall bladder, small intestine, and heart meridians.
▶ Steadies the energy, and gives a final "push" to the process of nadi purification begun in the other asanas.

Head, chest, and spine are straight, with the entire body facing forward

Right arm is stretching up, as though being pulled out from the waist

Arms are relaxed by the sides in preparation for the asana

Knees are straight, but relaxed

Do not allow the trunk to lean forward

Left arm is relaxing alongside the body

1 To come into the position, stand erect facing directly forward. Place the feet slightly more than shoulder width apart. Balance the weight of the body evenly between the two feet.

2 Inhale as you bring the right arm up alongside the right ear. Stretch the arm up as high as possible, and feel the stretch along the entire right side.

Stretches the muscles of the side of the body from the feet to the fingers

MAJOR BENEFIT

The Triangle gives an excellent, and complete, lateral stretch to the entire body. All the muscles are positively affected, especially those along the outer side of the body. These include the muscles of the ankles, legs, hips, and arms.

Right arm is straight and alongside the right ear

Eyes should be fixed straight ahead

3 Exhale as you bend to the left. Slide the left hand down the left leg as far as possible. Breathing regularly, hold the position for at least 30 seconds, and gradually increase to 1 minute. Return to the center and repeat on the other side. Perform this basic Triangle 2–5 times on each side.

COMMON PROBLEMS

▶ One or both knees are bent.

▶ Body is twisted forward or back.

▶ Upper elbow is bent.

▶ Head is dropped forward.

▶ Weight is mainly on one leg, rather than being evenly distributed.

▶ Weight is placed against the thigh by the lower hand.

▶ Eyes are looking downward.

Do not allow the body to twist

Left hand is resting gently on the outside of the left leg; imagine trying to grasp the ankle

Hand is placing weight against the thigh

TRIANGLE *Variations*

In its various permutations, the Triangle ensures a thorough lateral stretch to all parts of the body, promoting elasticity of the spine and helping to maintain a youthful posture.

VARIATION 1

This asana introduces a forward bend to the basic Triangle, stretching the body in a slightly different way.

Knees are straight, but do not try to tighten them

Left foot is turned out so that the two heels are now at a 90° angle to each other

1 Standing with the feet a little more than shoulder width apart, turn the left foot out. Clasp the hands behind the back and inhale deeply.

Elbows are kept straight as the arms are lifted

Hands are clasped together with the fingers loosely interwoven

Head and spine are kept in a straight line

2 Exhale and bend forward, bringing the forehead toward the left knee. Lift the arms as high as possible and hold the position for at least 10 seconds, gradually increasing to 1 minute. Inhale as you stand up to the starting position, and repeat on right side.

VARIATION 2

This relieves tension in shoulders that suffer from being hunched over a desk.

Hands are clasped loosely behind the back with the elbows straight

1 With the feet slightly more than shoulder width apart, take a big step to the left, bringing the feet as wide apart as is comfortable. Bend the left knee, and lunge to the left. Take a deep breath.

2 Exhale as you bring the forehead toward the floor just inside the left foot. Hold for at least 10 seconds, breathing gently. Gradually increase to 1 minute. Return to the starting position, and repeat by lunging to the right.

Left knee is bent, with the thigh parallel to the floor

Feet are flat on the floor and as wide apart as possible

Left foot is at a 90° angle to the right

Right knee is straight with the foot flat on the floor; do not allow the foot to rotate inward

VARIATION 3

This is a further variation in which the body is stretched in a deep lunge position. Practice on both sides.

Keep the body centered; do not lean to one side as you bend the knee

Right foot is flat on the floor

The body forms a straight line from the foot to the fingertips

1 ◁ With your feet a bit more than shoulder width apart, turn your left toes outward and bend the left knee. Bring your arms parallel to the floor at shoulder level.

The left knee is directly over the left foot

2 △ Place your left hand flat on the floor inside the left foot. Bring your right arm up next to your ear. Hold for 10 seconds, increasing to 1 minute.

Elbows are straight

Head and chest are held erect

Arms and shoulders are in a straight line

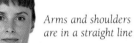

VARIATION 4

This apparently simple variation involves considerable chest and shoulder flexibility. Watch the alignment of arms and chest.

Legs are straight

1 ◁ Stand with the feet a little more than shoulder width apart. Raise the arms until they are held straight out from the shoulders.

2 ▽ Twisting from the hips, place the right hand flat on the floor outside the left foot. Align the body so that shoulders, chest, and arms form one straight line. Look up at the left hand. Hold for at least 10 seconds, and then repeat on the other side.

Right shoulder is directly over the right hand

FINAL RELAXATION

Just as it is important to begin every asana session with a period of relaxation, it is also essential to finish by spending about 10 minutes in the same way. The asanas tense and relax the various parts of the body, and to get the maximum benefit from them, it is important to give the physical, mental, and pranic energy an opportunity to circulate properly.

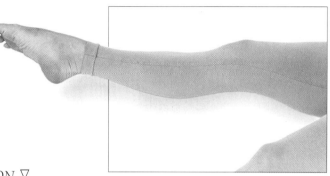

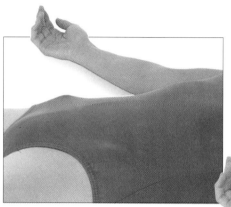

STARTING POSITION ▽

Lying flat on your back, bring the feet at least 1½ft (50cm) apart, and allow the toes to fall outward to the sides. Place the arms at an angle of approximately 45° to the body. Relax the hands, allowing the fingers to curl gently. Make your breathing very gentle and regular.

1 Raise the right leg 2in (5cm) from the floor, tense the muscles, and then release them, allowing the foot to fall gently to the floor. Raise the right leg, tense it, and allow it to drop.

2 Lift the right arm 2in (5cm) from the floor. Clench the hand, release the tension, and let the hand fall gently. Repeat with the left hand.

Legs are at least 1½ft (50cm) apart

Feet are relaxed with toes falling outward

Make sure that the calf muscles are relaxed

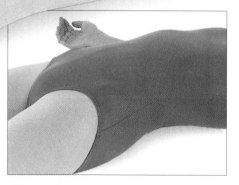

3 Lift the hips up from the floor, tense the buttocks by tightening them as much as possible, and release.

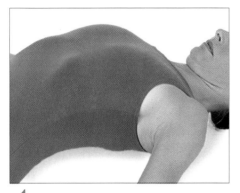

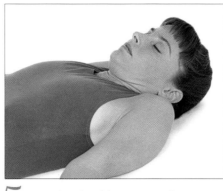

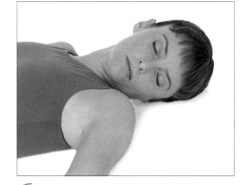

4 Raise the chest off the floor, tense it, and release. Allow it to fall back.

5 Raise the shoulders. Tense them, try to bring them together, and release.

6 Slowly roll the head from side to side, bringing one ear down to the floor, and then the other. Repeat this 2–3 times before returning to the center.

Breathe through the nose

Breathing is very gentle

7 Now begin the process of autosuggestion below. This should be done mentally. There is no need to move the body at all.

No energy is being used to keep the body in position

Arms are at 45° to the body

Hands are relaxed, with fingers slightly curled

AUTOSUGGESTION

▶ Beginning with the toes, feel as though a wave of relaxation is slowly moving up through the entire body. Mentally relax each toe, and then move on to the feet. Relax them completely.

▶ Feel the relaxation moving up the legs, relaxing the calves, the knees, and the thighs. Feel the relaxation coming up into the hips and the abdominal region. Relax all the internal organs.

▶ Relax the buttocks and feel the tension slowly releasing from each part of the back. Allow the floor to hold you up and, as the body relaxes, feel as though you are sinking down into it.

▶ Feel the relaxation coming into the chest, breathing very slowly and gently.

▶ Bring your attention to the fingers, relaxing each one in turn. Then relax the hands. Feel the relaxation moving up the arms, relaxing the wrists, forearms, and then the upper arms.

▶ Allow the shoulders to relax. Feel the wave of relaxation moving up the neck into the head.

▶ Relax the face and head. Begin with the jaw and let the mouth hang open slightly. Relax the tongue and the muscles at the back of the throat. Relax the chin and the cheeks, then the eyes and eyebrows, the forehead, and the scalp.

▶ Finally, relax the brain. All cares and worries are gone. Allow the mind and body to remain in this state of relaxation for at least 5 minutes more.

YOGIC BREATHING

"When the breath wanders, or is irregular, the mind is also unsteady, but when the breath is still, so is the mind, and the Yogi lives long. So one should restrain the breath."

Hatha Yoga Pradipika, 2-2

MENTAL & PHYSICAL ASPECTS OF BREATHING

No one can live for more than a few minutes without breathing,
but many people are unaware of the importance of breathing properly.
Bad mental and physical breathing habits mean that many of us use
only a fraction of our potential respiratory capacity.

RESPIRATION AND CIRCULATION

We derive our fuel from the food that we eat. Cells in
the body break down the chemicals in food into simpler
compounds, releasing energy and producing water and
carbon dioxide as waste products. This process, called
metabolism, requires oxygen. When we inhale, air fills
our lungs, and oxygen is absorbed into the bloodstream.
At the same time, the waste carbon dioxide passes from
the blood into the lungs to be exhaled. The oxygen-rich
blood returns to the heart and is then pumped to all
parts of the body to be used in metabolism.

MOVING OXYGEN

Oxygen is transported in the blood by the
red blood cells. These contain a protein
called hemoglobin, which binds with
oxygen and carries it in the bloodstream
to the parts of the body where it is
needed. The oxygen is then released
so that the body's cells can use it.

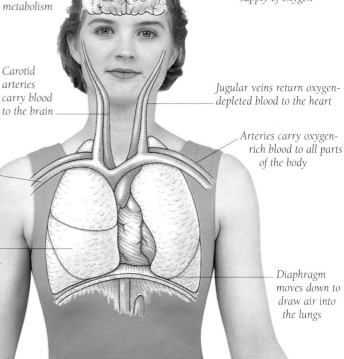

Neurons in the
brain have a
high rate of
metabolism

The brain
requires a rich
supply of oxygen

Carotid
arteries
carry blood
to the brain

Jugular veins return oxygen-
depleted blood to the heart

Arteries carry oxygen-
rich blood to all parts
of the body

Veins return
blood from
the body to
the heart

Exchange of
gases to and
from the blood
takes place in
the lungs

Diaphragm
moves down to
draw air into
the lungs

RED BLOOD CELLS
*The red cells in blood are packed
with hemoglobin, an iron-
containing protein that turns red
when combined with oxygen.*

MENTAL ASPECTS

Brain cells have a high rate of metabolism, so the brain requires much more oxygen, relatively, than any other organ of the body. The common remedy for stress is to take a deep breath; indeed, supplying the brain with sufficient oxygen is the greatest tool in stress management. A lack of oxygen means a loss of mental balance, concentration, and control of the emotions.

MENTAL BENEFITS OF PROPER BREATHING

SUN & MOON

▶ Improved concentration and greater clarity of thought.

▶ Increased ability to deal with complex situations without suffering from stress.

▶ Better emotional control and equilibrium.

▶ Improved physical control and coordination.

RIGHT SIDE OF THE BRAIN

Calming

Intuitive

Simultaneous

Holistic

Inner-directed

Emotional

Subjective

Feminine

Cool

Moon

Shakti

Yin

Ida Nadi

Spacial and nonverbal activities

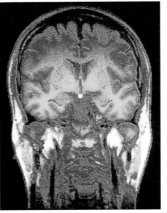

THE TWO BRAINS
As well as controlling opposite sides of the body, the two halves of the brain have specific functions and deal with different aspects of our lives. These lists show some of the characteristics of the two halves. Yogic breathing exercises help to keep the two sides of the brain in balance.

LEFT SIDE OF THE BRAIN

Aggressive

Logical

Sequential

Analytical

Outer-directed

Rational

Objective

Masculine

Hot

Sun

Siva

Yang

Pingala Nadi

Mathematical and verbal activities

PHYSICAL ASPECTS

Proper breathing demands a three-part movement. Firstly, the diaphragm causes the abdomen to expand, filling the lower lungs. Secondly, the intercostal muscles expand the rib cage and fill the middle lungs, and finally, the collar-bones lift, bringing air into the top part of the lungs. Most people breathe using only the top part of the lungs, literally starving the body of its essential oxygen, while preventing the complete elimination of noxious waste products.

PHYSICAL BENEFITS OF PROPER BREATHING

▶ Provides sufficient oxygen for the correct and efficient functioning of every body cell. Without sufficient oxygen, the cells cannot metabolize food properly. Nutrients, including precious vitamins and minerals, are wasted.

▶ Allows the body to rid itself of all the noxious gaseous by-products of metabolism, especially carbon dioxide.

GASEOUS EXCHANGE ▷
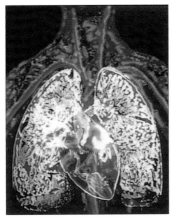
Oxygen is extracted from the air in the lungs, and passes into the blood through the walls of the lungs' air sacs. Gaseous waste products, collected from the cells and carried in the blood plasma, pass from the bloodstream into the lungs and are exhaled.

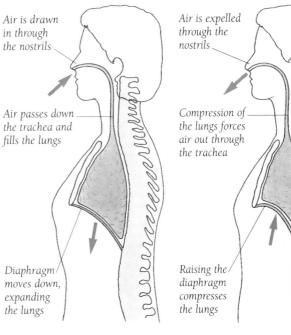

Air is drawn in through the nostrils

Air passes down the trachea and fills the lungs

Diaphragm moves down, expanding the lungs

Air is expelled through the nostrils

Compression of the lungs forces air out through the trachea

Raising the diaphragm compresses the lungs

INHALATION
Proper breathing is governed primarily by the movement of the diaphragm. As it descends, the abdomen expands, drawing fresh air in through the nose, through the trachea and bronchial tubes, and into the countless small air sacs inside the lungs.

EXHALATION
Yogic breathing places great importance on exhalation. As the diaphragm rises, the stale air is pushed out of the lungs with the help of the intercostal muscles, expelling various waste products from the body and counteracting the effects of pollution.

THE PRANIC BENEFITS OF YOGIC BREATHING

Breath is seen as the outward manifestation of prana, the vital force or energy that flows through the physical body but is actually in the astral body. By exercising control over breathing, you can learn to control the subtle energies within the body, and ultimately gain full control over the mind.

OUTWARD SIGNS OF THE INVISIBLE
We cannot see the wind, but we can infer its movements from the swaying of the trees. Prana, too, is invisible, but we can observe its state by looking at the state of the breath, since the breath is the outward manifestation of prana.

One of the seven chakras, or energy centers, that lie along the Sushumna

PRANIC BENEFITS
The prana, when consciously controlled, is a powerful, vitalizing and regenerating force. Once you are able to control the prana, it can be manipulated for self-development, for healing yourself of seemingly incurable diseases, and for healing others.

CHAKRAS AND NADIS
Seven energy centers, known as chakras, are located along the Sushumna, the central canal that corresponds to the spine in the physical body. The Pingala and Ida nadis, which flow through the right and left nostrils, run down each side of the Sushumna.

Pingala nadi

Ida nadi

The Sushumna nadi corresponds to the spinal cord in the physical body

THE CHAKRAS

The areas in the pranic sheath of the astral body (see p.8) where many nadis, or astral nerves, come together, are called chakras. Each chakra is like a telephone exchange, with many wires leading in and out. The chakras represent the vibratory levels of the astral body, becoming more subtle as they ascend. Through breathing exercises, or pranayama, the Yogi tries to raise his or her vibratory level. The energy pattern of each chakra is represented by particular colors and a certain number of lotus petals. Each petal bears one of the 50 letters of the Sanskrit alphabet, and one letter forms the central sound, or mantra.

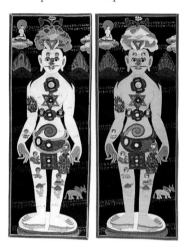

◁ CHAKRA CHARTS
Ancient depictions of the chakras show the Kundalini in the form of a coiled serpent. A coil represents potential energy, and the Kundalini is the spiritual potential that lies within each individual. Various Yogic techniques and exercises help practitioners to fulfill this spiritual potential.

THE NADIS

To the serious Yoga student, purification of the nadis is of the utmost importance in ensuring the healthy flow of the prana. An energy blockage in these astral tubes, or meridians, may result in physical and mental diseases, so Yoga exercises work in a similar way to acupuncture to purify and strengthen the nadis. Of the 72,000 nadis, the Sushumna, Ida, and Pingala are of prime importance to the Yogi. During ordinary activity, the majority of prana flows through either the Ida or Pingala. Only during meditation does it come into the Sushumna. Yoga breathing exercises help to balance the energies.

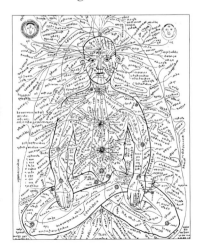

◁ MAP OF THE NADIS
Many ancient manuscripts show pictures of the energy patterns within the astral, or subtle, body. These are the nadis, the astral tubes that carry the prana, or vital energy. In acupuncture, they are referred to as meridians.

SAHASRARA CHAKRA
The seventh, highest, chakra is represented by a 1,000-petaled lotus, symbolizing the infinite.

AJNA CHAKRA
Located in the middle of the forehead, the third eye, as it is often called, has the mantra Om as its seed letter.

VISHUDDHA CHAKRA
As the fifth energy center in the astral body, Vishuddha is located at a point corresponding to the base of the throat.

The seed mantra of this chakra is Ham

ANAHATA CHAKRA
Use of the Anahata chakra, or heart center, as a focal point for meditation generates such pure qualities as cosmic love.

Two triangles, representing Siva and Shakti, contain the mantra Yam

MANIPURA CHAKRA
Located at the navel, Manipura corresponds to the solar plexus in the physical body.

A downward-pointing triangle contains the mantra Ram

SWADHISHTANA CHAKRA
The second chakra, shown with six petals, is situated along the Sushumna in the genital area.

A crescent moon contains the mantra Vam

MULADHARA CHAKRA
The lowest chakra, located at the base of the spine, is the resting place of the dormant Kundalini (spiritual potential).

This chakra's mantra is Lam

BREATHING EXERCISES

In Yogic breathing exercises, or pranayama, the breath is seen as the important link between our physical and mental aspects. Pranayama cleanses and strengthens the physical body, but its most important benefit is for the mind, which it calms, steadies, and clears.

ABDOMINAL BREATHING

Practice Abdominal Breathing lying flat on the back in the Corpse pose (see p.26). Become aware of the breath, which should be slow and deep. Make proper use of the diaphragm by drawing the air into the lowest and largest part of the lungs. As you inhale, feel the abdomen rise slowly. As you exhale, feel the abdomen sink down.

Feel the abdomen rise and fall as you breathe deeply

Face is relaxed; close the mouth and breathe gently through the nose

Feet and legs are relaxed

Hands are relaxed by the sides; you can place one hand on the abdomen to feel it rising and falling

It is important to keep the shoulders and neck relaxed

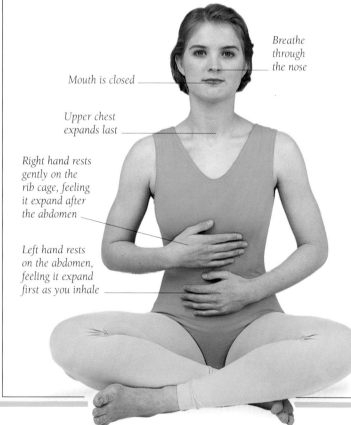

Breathe through the nose

Mouth is closed

Upper chest expands last

Right hand rests gently on the rib cage, feeling it expand after the abdomen

Left hand rests on the abdomen, feeling it expand first as you inhale

◁ FULL YOGIC BREATHING

To check that you are breathing correctly, sit in a cross-legged position with one hand on the abdomen and the other on the rib cage. Inhaling slowly, feel the abdomen expand first, then the rib cage, and finally feel the air filling the upper chest. As you exhale, the air will leave the lower lung first, then the middle, and lastly the top part. Practice this "proper" breathing on a regular basis.

FILLING THE LUNGS ▷

In Full Yogic Breathing, inhalation happens in three stages. Firstly, the diaphragm moves downward into the abdomen, drawing air into the lowest part of the lungs. Then the intercostal muscles expand the rib cage and pull air into the middle part of the lungs. Lastly, air comes into the upper part of the chest. This is called clavicular breathing.

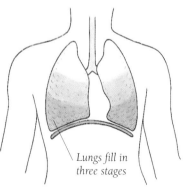

Lungs fill in three stages

ALTERNATE NOSTRIL BREATHING - *ANULOMA VILOMA*

The principal benefit of practicing Alternate Nostril Breathing, or Anuloma Viloma, is that it strengthens the respiratory system. Since exhalation is twice as long as inhalation, stale air and waste products are drained and expelled from the lungs and the entire body. Alternate Nostril Breathing calms and balances the mind; you should try to perform at least 10 rounds daily. Begin with the right hand in the Vishnu Mudra position and the thumb on the right nostril. When exhaling, try to empty the lungs completely.

Little and ring fingers are up

Middle and index fingers are bent into the palm

Thumb is up

VISHNU MUDRA

For this traditional hand position, bend the two middle fingers of the right hand into the palm. The thumb is used to close the right nostril. Place the two end fingers on the left nostril to close it.

1 Close the right nostril. Exhale through the left, and inhale to a count of 4.

2 Close the left nostril as well, and retain the breath to a count of 16.

3 Release the right nostril, and exhale fully through it to a count of 8.

4 Keeping the left nostril closed, inhale through the right to a count of 4.

5 Close both nostrils and retain the breath to a count of 16.

6 Release the left nostril, and exhale to a count of 8 to complete one round.

KEEPING COUNT

Use the left hand to count rounds, by touching each finger section in turn with the tip of the thumb.

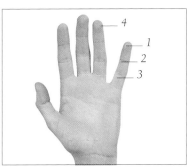

4
1
2
3

△ Start with the top section of the little finger. Ten rounds will bring you to the top of the index finger.

△ While counting the breathing rounds, rest the back of the left hand gently on the left knee.

PURIFICATION TECHNIQUES

As purity of body encourages purity of mind, Yogis have developed the six cleansing techniques, or Shad Kriyas, for purification of the physical body. Through these simple exercises, nature is assisted in the elimination of waste. You should not not attempt the Kriyas without the guidance of a teacher.

NASAL CLEANSING - NETI

Neti cleanses the nose, nasal passages, and sinus cavities. Practiced daily, this purification exercise helps to counteract the effects of pollution, dust, and pollen. It is especially beneficial to people with asthma, allergies, and other respiratory problems.

Solution of ½ teaspoon of sea salt in a cup of lukewarm tap water

CERAMIC NETI WATER PITCHER

BRASS NETI WATER PITCHER

PERFORMING NASAL CLEANSING
Tip your head to the left and hold your breath. Use a neti jug to pour water into the right nostril and out of the left. Blow your nose and repeat on the other side.

COLON CLEANSING - BASTI

Basti cleans the lower large intestine by creating a vacuum that draws water up into it. While sitting in a tub of water, create the vacuum by manipulating your abdominal muscles (Nauli – see opposite page). Traditionally a small bamboo tube was used to keep the anal sphincter open. A modern alternative is a small plastic tube with a diameter of about ½in (1cm). Basti is not the same thing as an enema, which relies on pressure to introduce water into the lower intestine. The practice of basti strengthens the abdominal muscles, rather than weakening them, so it can be performed on a regular basis.

STOMACH CLEANSING - DHAUTI

Dhauti cleanses the esophagus and stomach by removing excess mucus and food left on the stomach walls. Use a 16ft (5m) roll of 2in (5cm) gauze soaked in a solution of diluted sea salt and tap water (as for Neti). At first, swallow only 1ft (30cm), gradually increasing each time until you can swallow the full length.

BOWL OF SALTWATER SOLUTION

1 Place one end of the gauze in the mouth and begin chewing, to stimulate the swallow response. Chew and swallow until just a short length remains out of the mouth.

SEA SALT   *2IN (5CM) GAUZE*

2 Keep the cloth in the stomach for a few minutes, ideally performing Nauli to cleanse the stomach walls. Then pull the gauze out. Practice Dhauti twice a week on an empty stomach.

ABDOMINAL CHURNING - *NAULI*

Nauli massages and invigorates all the internal organs, and also brings a concentration of prana to the solar plexus region. A powerful tonic for any gastrointestinal disorder or weakness, it may take some time to master, as various abdominal muscles need to be brought under control. Begin by standing with legs apart, knees slightly bent, and hands resting on the thighs. Practicing Nauli regularly greatly improves the posture, as well as strengthening the muscles that are used for breathing and for elimination.

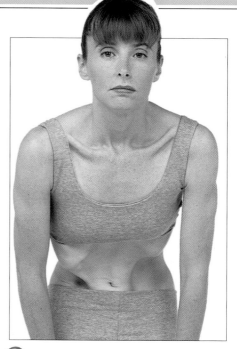

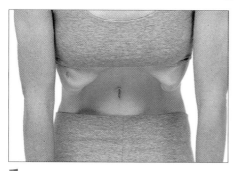

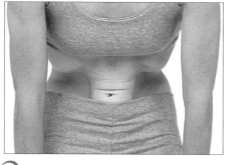

1 Stand up, bending forward slightly, with your hands on your thighs. Take a deep breath and exhale fully, pushing on the thighs. When the lungs are empty, draw the diaphragm upward.

2 Without taking a breath, contract the central band of muscles in the abdomen and push it forward, forming a ridge down the center of the abdomen. Draw the muscles in and out.

3 Once you have mastered central Nauli, try abdominal churning. Press harder on the thigh with the right hand to move the muscle to the left, and vice versa. Try to produce a smooth, wavelike motion.

RESPIRATORY SYSTEM CLEANSE - *KAPALABHATI*

This breathing exercise purifies the nasal passage and the lungs, helping the body eliminate large quantities of carbon dioxide and other impurities. The added intake of oxygen enriches the blood and renews body tissues, while the movement of the diaphragm massages the stomach, liver, and pancreas.

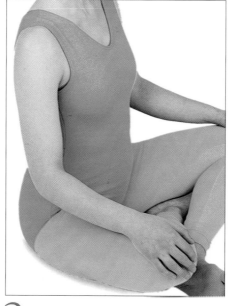

1 Contract the abdominal muscles quickly, causing the diaphragm to rise and force the air out of the lungs.

2 Relax the abdomen, allowing the air to return gently to the lungs. Repeat 20–50 times quickly for 3–5 rounds.

STEADY GAZING - *TRATAK*

Placing a candle an arm's length away at eye level, gaze at the flame without blinking for 1–3 minutes. Your eyes will water, cleansing the eyes and the tear ducts. Then close your eyes and picture the flame at a point between the eyebrows. Tratak improves eyesight and concentration, and can be used as a preliminary exercise for meditation.

IMPROVING CONCENTRATION

PROPER
RELAXATION

When the mind, body, and senses are
continually bombarded with stimuli, they have
no chance to rejuvenate themselves. In order
to achieve radiant health and well-being, a
time must be set aside each day to allow
this rejuvenation to take place.

RELAXATION OR TENSION?

True relaxation is experienced by the body and mind when little or no energy is consumed. It is nature's way of recharging. Since every action, conscious or unconscious, uses stored energy, relaxation is necessary for good health and peace of mind. Without proper relaxation, the body and mind become overworked and inefficient.

ACTION MEANS USING ENERGY

To understand the principle of relaxation, it is helpful to understand its opposite. All action creates stress and, although no one can live without some stress, undue tensions wear out the body and mind. Every action involves several stages. First of all, stimuli are taken in through the senses and are transmitted via the nervous system to the mind. The mind then analyzes the stimuli and decides what action, if any, is to be taken. The mind sends an impulse to the muscles involved, along with an extra supply of energy for performing the action. The impulse, enforced by the energy, causes the muscles to contract and act. Many aspects of modern life make it increasingly difficult to relax. We are so bombarded with stimuli that most people unknowingly waste enormous amounts of energy. One of the keys to relaxation is to reduce the number of stimuli to which we are subjected.

WORKING CONDITIONS
In a modern lifestyle, the mind and muscles are kept tense all the time. This can deplete large amounts of stored energy, causing a variety of stress-related symptoms.

ENTERTAINMENT
Movies, television, and some spectator sports are full of violence. Many of us regard these as relaxing, but in fact they have a contrary effect, tending to overstimulate the emotions.

SOCIAL LIFE ▷
Alcohol, drugs, and loud music are common forms of recreation, but they are not relaxing. They leave the body even more tense, craving ever larger doses to gain momentary relief.

PHYSICAL RELAXATION

Exercise can increase the body's energy, but it is futile if energy is constantly being wasted by keeping the muscles in a state of readiness. Some people have trained their muscles to be so tense that they can't relax them even at night, and there is a constant energy drain. Then, exercising is like trying to fill a leaking bucket.

Yoga asanas are a technique for retraining the muscles to be able to relax. People who practice asanas often find that they need less sleep and feel more rested. This is because they can quickly fall into a sound sleep. Deep sleep rejuvenates body and mind, but light sleep, or the dream state, actually uses energy.

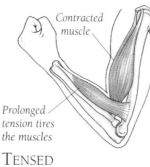

Contracted muscle

Well-trained muscles relax when they are not working

Prolonged tension tires the muscles

TENSED
We tend to use more energy keeping the muscles ready for work than in actually doing useful work. This puts undue stress upon the muscles, and they become unable to relax.

RELAXED
If the muscles are allowed to relax between work, rather than being kept tense, they will perform more efficiently.

MENTAL RELAXATION

When the mind is constantly bombarded by stimuli, it becomes overloaded and exhausted. We may be unaware that we are doing it, but by thinking and worrying we are using up tremendous amounts of energy. The tension put on the mind by worries, whether real or imagined, can use more energy than physical work. When worries get out of hand, energy resources are strained. Mental fatigue sets in, often resulting in wear and tear on the physical body as well. It is important to set aside some time each day for the mind to unwind and recoup its energies.

Whenever you experience mental tension, try breathing slowly and rhythmically for a few minutes while you concentrate on the breath. Yogic breathing exercises will develop your ability to calm the mind using your own thought power. This leads to an experience of inner peace, with physical relaxation following the mental relaxation.

KEEPING UP THE PACE
Trying to keep up with the fast pace and complexity of modern life results in the unthinking wasting of stored-up energy. The body and mind are denied the opportunity to recharge.

MENTAL WORK
Efficiency comes when a person is able to relax while engaged in the work at hand. At first, this may take conscious effort, but you will soon establish a positive habit. Asanas, pranayama, and meditation all train the body and mind to relax and concentrate.

SPIRITUAL RELAXATION

Complete mental and physical relaxation come only with an inner tuning to a higher source. As long as we identify with this body and mind, we all think we can rely on no one but ourselves. There will always be tension and worries about the future. Tuning to the divine source brings the realization that all happiness comes from within. Yoga gives the techniques for this inner tuning, enabling us to break down the boundaries that separate us from one another, and from our own inner selves.

ONENESS
Through meditation, we can achieve an experience of Oneness that destroys emotions such as jealousy, anger, fear, and hatred at their roots.

MEDITATION
It is the nature of the mind to jump constantly, using up large amounts of energy. In meditation, the rays of the mind are focused and we experience absolute silence and peace. This gives a profound inner relaxation to the body and mind, relieving all stress.

RELAXATION TECHNIQUES

Although relaxation is usually perceived as merely a physical condition, it actually has roots that extend into the astral body, and even more deeply into the causal body. This is why attempts to relax only the physical body with alcohol or drugs do not succeed. Proper complete relaxation comes only when the body, mind, and spirit are all at ease.

RELAXATION POSES

Asanas work with the mind as well as the physical body. Using concentration, asanas retrain the muscles to act in a relaxed manner. Certain relaxation poses are also done before, between, and after the other asanas, to ensure a proper flow of prana (vital energy) within the body.

CHILD'S POSE ▷

Sit on the heels with knees and feet together, forehead on the ground. Rest the hands on the ground, palms up, by the feet. Breathing gently through the nose, sink down into the position.

◁ CORPSE POSE

Lie flat on the back, with the legs at least 1½ft (50cm) apart. Place the arms at an angle of about 45° to the body. No energy should be expended to hold the body in this position. Focus the mind on the breath. Feel the abdomen rise as you inhale and sink as you exhale.

RELAXING ON THE ABDOMEN ▷

Lying on your front, place one hand on top of the other, turn the head, and rest one cheek on the hands. Close the eyes and breathe deeply, as in the Corpse pose, feeling the abdomen press into the ground as you inhale, and rise as you exhale.

BREATHING TO RELAX

Yogic breathing techniques use the breath as a tool to help strengthen the control of the mind over the body. Several times a day, run a mental check on your body. If you find tension in any area, consciously let go of it. "Breathe" it out of your body using autosuggestion. For example, every time you inhale, imagine that you are drawing prana in from the air. That prana may be consciously directed to any part of the body. With each exhalation, feel that a little tension is leaving the body. When breathing is not full, the brain is the first organ to suffer, and stressful situations develop more easily. Always remember to "take a deep breath" when under any pressure.

FULL YOGIC BREATH

The whole volume of the lungs is used for Full Yogic Breathing (see p.112), taking in the maximum amount of air, and providing the body with as much oxygen as possible. This allows all the cells, tissues, and organs to maintain peak performance levels, rather than becoming depleted and stressed. Full Yogic Breathing also rids the body of poisonous waste gases as efficiently as possible.

STRESS-FREE DIET

What, when, where, and how you eat all have an important bearing on the relaxed (or stressed) state of your body and mind. Eat slowly and in a relaxed manner. Don't overload the system. Keep your diet simple and nutritious, in accordance with the principles described in the Vegetarian Diet chapter (see pp.124–151). A meat-free diet, high in fiber, fresh fruits, and vegetables, puts the least stress on your system, while fulfilling all the essential energy requirements. Eat at regular mealtimes, and not in between. Don't eat before going to sleep.

A wholesome vegetarian diet provides all the right ingredients for a healthy body and mind

EAT IN MODERATION

Overeating is the chief cause of many diseases, especially those of the circulatory and digestive systems. It can truly be said that most people dig their graves with their teeth. The Yogic ideal is to fill the stomach half full of food, a quarter full of liquid, and to leave the last quarter empty, so that digestion can proceed unhampered. Yogis believe that the secret of being both healthy and happy is to be a little hungry at all times.

RELAXATION IN SLEEP

Despite sleeping for up to 12 hours per night, many people still wake up feeling exhausted. This is because they are unable to enter easily into a deep sleep, which is the restful state. If you have trouble falling asleep or find it difficult to have a good night's rest, try to relax the body and mind completely using autosuggestion. Lie in bed and go through the Final Relaxation steps (see pp.104–5).

DREAM STATE
In light sleep, or the dream state, energy is being used rather than generated.

DEEP SLEEP
In deep sleep the body has the best opportunity to rejuvenate itself.

MENTAL ATTITUDE

It is important to realize that the main stresses in life come not from outside situations, but from your own mental and emotional reaction to them. Through the practice of pranayama, asanas, and meditation, you will be able to control the mind and keep it as tension-free as possible. Positive thinking (see pp.154–5) is the ability to stand back and be a silent witness. This can often mean dealing with the situation, rather than with your own emotional reaction to it. Maintaining the proper mental attitude enables you to cope with a potentially stressful situation. Then you can transform it into an educational, and even an enjoyable, experience.

RELAX IN SILENCE

A considerable amount of energy is used up in talk and socializing. Most people never realize the truth of this. Even when they are alone, they tend to sit in front of the television, which has the effect of stimulating the senses rather than recharging them. There is no better healing balm than silence. It soothes nerves wounded by turmoil, friction, and rupture, and relieves the stresses of daily life.

A QUIET TIME
For your mental and physical well-being, it is important to set aside some time each day when you are able to be peaceful and by yourself. Sit quietly, read, listen to music of an inspirational nature, or engage the mind in a focused, yet relaxing, activity.

VEGETARIAN DIET

To the Yogi, the body is a mold prepared by the mind to carry out the activities of the mind. The foods that we eat to build both the body and the mind should therefore be pure, wholesome, and nutritious.

WHAT WE NEED FROM FOOD

The human body needs food for two purposes – as fuel for energy, and as raw material to repair itself. A natural vegetarian diet provides the fuel that keeps the body functioning at its best, gives the most energy, and contains the fewest additives.

ENERGY FOR LIVING

Our bodies need to take in fuel, in the form of food, at regular intervals. This is digested in the stomach and intestines, which break it down into usable forms. The nutrients are absorbed in the intestines and transported through the bloodstream to all the cells of the body.

PROPER DIET
Food has several basic components, such as fiber, carbohydrates, and vitamins. All of these are essential if the body is to function at its best.

THE SUN
Our energy originates from the sun. The closer to the source we are able to eat, the more potent the energy. Only prana and vitamin D can be derived directly from the sun by humans.

PLANTS
By the process of photosynthesis, plants are able to convert solar energy into matter. Cereals, such as corn, are able to store the energy in a form that is readily assimilated and easy to use.

VEGETARIANS
Animals cannot take their energy directly from the sun; they must obtain it via plants. Vegetarian animals, including humans, are adapted to assimilate plants and take in their energy secondhand.

CARNIVORES
Meat eaters receive their energy thirdhand. Energy is lost at each level in the food pyramid, and the energy that carnivores derive from their food is less potent than the energy vegetarians derive.

FIBER

Dietary fiber is the indigestible part of the plants in our diet. It is essential for health because it speeds the passage of food through the digestive system and absorbs harmful substances. Meat contains no dietary fiber, and refining processes remove the fiber from whole foods. Low fiber intake contributes to many modern ailments.

FIBER-RICH
Dietary fiber is found in many vegetables, fruits, and cereals.

CARROTS

PINTO BEANS

DRIED APRICOTS

OAT FLAKES

BLUEBERRIES

BROWN RICE

BANANA

WHOLE WHEAT BREAD

PROTEINS

These nitrogen-containing compounds are necessary for building tissues and repairing cells. The breakdown of protein creates nitrogenous wastes, and the body has to eliminate these. Some meat products, such as offal, are particularly high in certain kinds of protein; however, the process of removing these from the body can place a strain on the kidneys, reducing their efficiency and leading to problems in later life.

CHEESE

NUTS

SUNFLOWER SEEDS

PEARL BARLEY

PUMPKIN SEEDS

KIDNEY BEANS

PROTEIN FACTS

Proteins are made up of 20 "building blocks" called amino acids. Eating a variety of protein foods provides all the necessary amino acids. Contrary to popular belief, a fully vegetarian diet (left) does provide enough protein – meat eaters may get too much!

FATS

Fats provide the body with a reserve of energy. Small quantities of fat enable the body to store vital fat-soluble vitamins, such as vitamins A, D, E, and K. The body also needs fat to build and maintain cushions for the internal organs, and to make the protective myelin sheaths that enclose the nerves.

NERVE IN MYELIN SHEATH

OILS

AVOCADO

SOYBEANS

CORN

OLIVES

PEANUTS

FAT FACTS

Fats are made up of saturated and unsaturated fatty acids. Regular consumption of saturated fatty acids – found mainly in animal products – overloads the system and can cause heart disease. The fatty acids in nuts, fruit, and vegetables (left) are almost all unsaturated.

CARBOHYDRATES

These compounds are the chemical form in which plants store energy, and carbohydrates are recommended as the main energy source in the diet. Simple carbohydrates can be broken down completely to provide energy. Other more complex compounds (including some kinds of starch) cannot be digested, and these act like dietary fiber, helping to keep the intestines healthy.

WHOLE-GRAIN BREAD

ARBORIO RICE

POTATOES

PASTA

CHICK PEAS

CALORIE FACTS

Many carbohydrates are broken down into sugars in the digestive system. They are best eaten unrefined (left) as they also provide other nutrients. Foods that contain only simple carbohydrates, such as refined sugar, candy, and alcohol, provide only empty calories.

VITAMINS AND MINERALS

Small amounts of these are vital for the proper functioning of the body. Plants produce vitamins, and they also take in minerals, so a balanced vegetarian diet provides sufficient quantities of these essential ingredients.

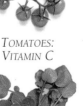

CELERY: SODIUM

BLUEBERRIES: VITAMIN C

TOMATOES: VITAMIN C

LEMONS: VITAMIN C

ASPARAGUS: FOLATE

WATERCRESS: POTASSIUM

CARROT JUICE: VITAMIN A

RED PEPPERS: IRON

VITAMIN FACTS

There are vegetarian sources (left) for all essential vitamins and minerals, but all fruits and vegetables should be eaten as fresh and as raw as possible. Overcooking and processing can deplete even the most nutritious food of these vital components.

WHY BE VEGETARIAN?

The Yogi sees the body as a vehicle for the soul, and therefore treats it with the utmost respect and care. Every effort is made to understand the underlying principles that permeate all life, the essential unity of the diverse forms in the world. To keep this tuning, simple vegetarian food is eaten, supplying essential energy while maintaining purity of body and mind.

CONSIDER YOUR HEALTH

The human digestive system functions best on a vegetarian diet. Vegetarians have very low cholesterol levels and fewer heart problems. They have a 40% lower incidence of cancer, and are less likely to suffer from arthritis, obesity, diet-related diabetes, constipation, gallstones, high blood pressure, food poisoning, and many other ailments.

KEY TO FOODS
■ MEAT
■ FISH
■ LEGUMES
■ VEGETABLES & FRUIT

THE CONTENT OF FOODS
In this chart the colored blocks indicate the fat, fiber, and cholesterol content of various foods. The scale ranges from one block (very low content) to four blocks (high content). The chart shows that vegetarian foods contain hardly any fat or cholesterol, and are high in fiber, which is virtually absent from animal products.

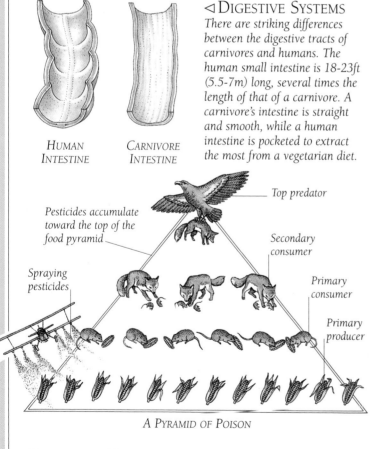

◁ DIGESTIVE SYSTEMS
There are striking differences between the digestive tracts of carnivores and humans. The human small intestine is 18-23ft (5.5-7m) long, several times the length of that of a carnivore. A carnivore's intestine is straight and smooth, while a human intestine is pocketed to extract the most from a vegetarian diet.

HUMAN INTESTINE   CARNIVORE INTESTINE

Pesticides accumulate toward the top of the food pyramid

Top predator
Secondary consumer
Primary consumer
Primary producer
Spraying pesticides

A PYRAMID OF POISON

POLLUTION PYRAMID
The many chemicals, pesticides, and antibiotics sprayed on crops are eaten by animals. These become more concentrated the higher up the food chain you eat – an effect known as bio-amplification.

FOOD FAT CONTENT	FAT	FIBER	CHOLESTEROL
■ BACON	4	1	4
■ LAMB CHOP	4	1	4
■ SALAMI	3	–	3
■ SAUSAGE	3	–	3
■ CHICKEN	2	–	3
■ STEAK	2	–	3
■ GROUND BEEF	2	1	3
■ VEAL	1	–	4
■ ANCHOVIES	2	–	3
■ MACKEREL	2	–	4
■ SARDINES	2	–	3
■ HERRING	2	–	2
■ AVOCADO	2	3	1
■ TUNA	1	–	3
■ SALMON	2	–	2
■ SOYBEANS	2	3	1
■ TOFU	2	3	–
■ SHRIMP	1	–	4
■ LETTUCE	1	2	–
■ ASPARAGUS	1	2	–
■ MUSHROOMS	1	2	1
■ GREEN BEANS	1	2	1
■ BEAN SPROUTS	1	2	1
■ BANANAS	1	2	1
■ CELERY	1	2	1
■ POTATOES	1	2	1
■ CABBAGE	1	3	1
■ FAVA BEANS	1	3	1
■ LENTILS	1	2	1
■ LIMA BEANS	1	2	1
■ KIDNEY BEANS	1	3	1
■ DRIED APRICOTS	1	4	1

ETHICS AND ECOLOGY

There are many ethical reasons for being vegetarian. When practicing Yoga, one of the most important is the principle of ahimsa, or nonviolence. As the first of the yamas of Raja Yoga (see p.7), the practice of noninjury to all living things must be followed at all times. Nonviolence toward fellow beings must be extended to include noninjury of the environment if the planet is to be protected. There are far too many examples of wanton destruction.

RESPECT ANIMALS
All of the fear and pain of a slaughtered animal is taken into our bodies when we eat its meat, and this makes our own emotions increasingly difficult to control.

RESPECT THE EARTH
An area of the world's rain forest greater than the size of New York State is destroyed each year, largely to create grazing land for food animals.

FINANCIAL SENSE

Meat production is a highly expensive and wasteful process. When legumes and grains are converted into meat by feeding them to animals, 90% of the protein, 96% of the energy value, all the fiber, and all the carbohydrates are lost. The price of meat reflects this waste.

EXPENSIVE TASTES
A meat-based diet costs far more than a vegetarian diet and is nutritionally far poorer. For the price of two lamb chops, you can buy the ingredients for a complete vegetarian dinner of soup, salad, main course, and dessert for one person. The vegetarian option is nutritionally balanced and far more healthful.

POLITICAL REASONS

There are some 800 million hungry people in the world today. Every two seconds, a child dies from malnutrition. Up to 60 million people in developing countries die annually from hunger and hunger-related diseases. Food in poorer countries is systematically being fed to animals so that meat can be sold to the more prosperous nations. At the same time, people in the so-called "developed" countries spend enormous sums of money every year on dietary products, because their food intake is excessively high. In a world with limited productive land, it makes no sense to produce meat when the land could feed many more people if used to grow cereals or legumes.

BEEF FEEDS ONLY ONE ▷
12.5 acres (5 hectares) of land is needed to grow the food to supply the needs of each person eating a meat-based diet.

ONE!   BEEF

CORN FEEDS FIVE ▷
12.5 acres (5 hectares) of land could feed five people if corn were grown for human consumption rather than for animal feed.

CORN FEEDS FIVE   CORN

SOY FEEDS 30 ▽
A soybean crop from 12.5 acres (5 hectares) would provide the most energy, feeding 30 people.

WHEAT FEEDS 12 ▷
If wheat were to be grown on 12.5 acres (5 hectares) of land, the crop would feed 12 people.

WHEAT FEEDS 12 PEOPLE   WHEAT

A SOYBEAN CROP WOULD FEED 30 PEOPLE   SOYBEANS

YOU ARE WHAT YOU EAT

Yoga develops our pure inner nature, and diet plays an important part in this process. The Yogic scriptures divide food into three types: sattvic, or pure; rajasic, or stimulating; and tamasic, or impure and rotten. The Yogic diet is based on pure, sattvic foods.

OVERACTIVITY - *RAJAS*

The Yogic diet avoids substances that are overstimulating, or rajasic. Onions, garlic, coffee, tea, and tobacco are rajasic, as are heavily spiced and salted items, and many fast foods and snacks. Refined sugar, soft drinks, and chocolate are also rajasic. Rajasic foods arouse animal passions, bring a restless state of mind, and make the person overactive. They destroy the mind/body balance that is essential for happiness.

RAJASIC BEHAVIOR
Rajasic foods overstimulate the body and mind, cause physical and mental stress, and encourage circulatory and nervous disorders.

RAJASIC FOODS
"The foods that are bitter, sour, saline, excessively hot, pungent, dry, and burning, are liked by the rajasic and are productive of pain, grief, and disease."
Bhagavad Gita, 17-9

INERTIA - *TAMAS*

Tamasic substances are avoided in the Yogic diet because they produce feelings of heaviness and lethargy. Meat, fish, eggs, drugs, and alcohol are tamasic, as are overcooked and packaged foods. Other tamasic items include those that have been fermented, burned, fried, barbecued, or reheated many times, as well as stale products or those containing preservatives. Mushrooms are considered tamasic, since they grow in darkness.

TAMASIC BEHAVIOR
A tamasic diet benefits neither body nor mind. It makes a person dull and lazy, lacking in high ideals, purpose, and motivation. Such individuals tend to suffer from chronic ailments and from depression. Overeating is tamasic.

TAMASIC FOODS
"That food which is stale, tasteless, putrid, rotten, and impure refuse, is the food liked by the tamasic."
Bhagavad Gita, 17-10

THE RULES OF EATING

"Purity of mind depends on purity of food." – Swami Sivananda

▶ Try to keep your meals on a regular schedule, but if you do not feel hungry at mealtime, fast until the next meal.

▶ Eat slowly, and savor your food. Chew it thoroughly, remembering that digestion begins in the mouth.

▶ Eat only four or five different foods at one meal. Complex mixtures are difficult to digest. Do not snack between meals.

▶ Do not overload your system. Fill half the stomach with food, one quarter with liquid, and leave the rest empty.

▶ Maintain a peaceful attitude during the meal. Try to eat in silence.

▶ Change your diet gradually.

▶ Before you eat, remember God, who dwells in all foods and who bestows all bounties.

▶ Try to fast for one day a week.

▶ Eat at least one raw salad every day.

▶ Eat to live – don't live to eat.

PURITY - *SATTVA*

The Yogic diet consists of sattvic foods that calm the mind and sharpen the intellect. These are pure, wholesome, and naturally delicious, without preservatives or artificial flavorings. They include fresh and dried fruits and berries, pure fruit juices, raw or lightly cooked vegetables, salads, grains, legumes, nuts, seeds, whole-grain breads, honey, fresh herbs, herbal teas, and dairy products such as milk and butter. A sattvic diet is easily digested and supplies maximum energy, increasing vitality, strength, and endurance. It will help eliminate fatigue, even for those who undertake strenuous and difficult work. Yogis believe that people's food preferences reflect their level of mental purity and that these preferences alter as they develop spiritually.

SATTVIC FOODS

"The foods which increase life, purity, strength, health, joy, and cheerfulness, which are savory and oleaginous, substantial and agreeable, are dear to the sattvic people."
Bhagavad Gita, 17-8

SATTVIC BEHAVIOR

A sattvic diet brings purity and calmness to the mind, and is both soothing and nourishing to the body. It promotes cheerfulness, serenity, and mental clarity, and helps maintain mental poise and nervous equilibrium throughout the day.

SOUPS

Soups are nourishing, satisfying, and very easy to make. They provide an economical way to feed a large family, using simple ingredients, as well as being an easily prepared meal for busy people. A variety of vegetables can be used: in winter, root vegetables such as parsnips, turnips, and rutabagas make a warming broth, especially with the addition of grains or beans. For a light summer soup, use watercress, tomatoes, zucchini, and lettuce, and flavor with fresh herbs.

POTAGE CRESSONIÈRE

A delightful soup to serve cool for dinner on hot summer evenings.

INGREDIENTS
3 medium potatoes
5 cups (1.25 liters) water
1 cup (225ml) milk or cream (optional)
½ bunch watercress
¼ teaspoon grated nutmeg
salt and pepper

Peel and dice the potatoes, and place them in a large pan. Cover with cold water, bring to a boil, and simmer with the lid on for about 8–10 minutes, or until the potatoes are tender. Drain the potatoes and transfer to a large bowl, reserving the cooking water. Mash the potatoes until smooth, adding milk or cream if desired. Chop the watercress after washing it thoroughly. Return the potatoes to the pan with the cooking water, and add the chopped watercress and grated nutmeg. Stir well, bring to a low boil, and simmer for 10 minutes. Season to taste with salt and pepper, adding more milk if the soup appears too thick. This soup can be served hot, but you may prefer to serve it chilled, as a very simple, elegant, and healthy dish. For the chilled version, allow the soup to cool, and place in a refrigerator until ready to serve. *Serves 4.*

POTAGE CRESSONIÈRE

CORN CHOWDER

A thick creamy soup that can be a meal in itself when served with whole-grain bread and salad.

INGREDIENTS
4 fresh ears of corn
¼ cabbage, shredded
3 medium potatoes, diced
3½ cups (850ml) cold water
¾ cup (175ml) soy milk
salt and pepper

Scrape the kernels off the corn. Place in a pan with the cabbage and potatoes. Cover with water. Bring to a boil and simmer, covered, until the potatoes are soft. Blend, then add the soy milk, and season to taste with salt and pepper. Reheat gently, but do not boil. Serve immediately. *Serves 4.*

VEGETABLE SOUP

This is a very easy soup to make for any number of people. Simply multiply the ingredients by the number of diners.

INGREDIENTS (PER PERSON)
½ tablespoon oil
8oz (200g) diced mixed vegetables
1 cup (200ml) water
½ cup (50g) spinach or seasonal greens, roughly shredded
salt or tamari to taste

Heat the oil in a pan, and sauté the vegetables. Add the water, and bring to boil. Cover with a lid, and simmer for 20 minutes. Add the spinach or greens, and cook for another 5 minutes. Season with salt or tamari and serve. *Serves any number.*

MISO SOUP

Different types of miso add different flavors to food: light miso is fragrant and sweet; red-brown miso is aromatic and tasty; dark miso is pungent and salty. Always buy the best: you use so little, and it is worth the expense for a better flavor.

INGREDIENTS

2 teaspoons vegetable oil
2 teaspoons grated fresh ginger
1½lb (700g) chopped or sliced vegetables,
e.g., cabbage, celery, carrots, potatoes,
rutabagas, parsnip, turnip, kale
1 tablespoon dried wakame seaweed
4 cups (1 liter) water
or vegetable stock
4 tablespoons light miso
2 tablespoons finely chopped parsley

Heat the oil in a large wok or heavy pan. Add the ginger and vegetables, and sauté for 5 minutes. Meanwhile, soak the wakame for 4–6 minutes, then chop roughly. Add the water or stock, and chopped wakame, to the vegetables in a pan. Cover and bring to a boil, then reduce the heat and simmer for 15 minutes, or until the vegetables are just tender. Cream the miso with about 8 tablespoons of the broth; stir into the broth and remove the pan from the heat. Serve immediately, garnished with chopped parsley. Do not reheat miso soup.
Serves 4–6.

TOMATO SOUP

MISO SOUP

SOUP-MAKING METHODS

▶ One basic soup-making method involves chopping the vegetables finely, and then sautéing them lightly in butter or oil. This draws out the flavor of the vegetables. When the vegetables are softened, add the water and seasonings, such as bay leaf, salt, and pepper. Bring the soup to a boil, then reduce the heat and simmer for approximately 25 minutes.

▶ An alternative, simpler method is to add water directly to the raw, chopped vegetables, together with the seasonings. Bring to a boil, reduce the heat, and then simmer for approximately 25 minutes.

▶ For a heartier soup, you can add beans or peas, but you may have to soak these first and the soup will require a longer cooking time – up to 1 hour.

▶ Adding miso before serving is a convenient way of adding extra flavor and nutrition. Made from beans and/or grain, it is an excellent source of protein. In Japan, miso is used to cure colds and to clear the skin. Miso is a living organism, rather like yeast, so it should never be boiled or recooked.

TOMATO SOUP

This simple soup is best made using fresh tomatoes, flavored with Mediterranean herbs.

INGREDIENTS

2 tablespoons oil
1 green pepper, finely chopped
2 sticks celery, finely chopped
1 carrot, grated
1 teaspoon dried oregano
1½ teaspoons dried basil
28oz (800g) canned or 2lb (1kg) fresh tomatoes, chopped
1½ teaspoons salt
black pepper
2 cups (570ml) hot water or vegetable stock

Heat the oil in a large pan, and sauté the chopped vegetables over a medium heat for 5 minutes. Stir in the herbs, and cook for another 2 minutes. Add the tomatoes, salt, and pepper, and bring to a boil. Pour in the hot water or stock, bring back to the boil, and then simmer for 20 minutes. Season to taste, and serve immediately.
Serves 6.

VARIATIONS: For a thicker consistency, add some flour with the vegetables, and stir well as you add the water or stock. For a creamy tomato soup, mix milk or soy milk with a little soup when it is cooked, and then return to the pan, stirring well. Reheat gently, but do not boil. For an even heartier tomato soup, add 1 cup (150g) of cooked grain at the same time as the water or stock.

SALADS, DIPS, AND DRESSINGS

As a complement to main courses, or as meals in their own right, salads of raw fruit and vegetables should form a major part of any diet, whether vegetarian or other. They are an important source of vitamins, minerals, bulk, and fiber, and they add variety, texture, and flavor to any meal. Garnishing with sprouting seeds (such as alfalfa, mung beans, or lentils), nuts, wheat germ, seeds (including sesame, sunflower, and caraway), or even nutritional yeast, can produce unlimited variations.

BASIC SALAD DRESSING

This simple dressing will add zest to any salad and takes only minutes to prepare.

INGREDIENTS
¼ cup (55ml) vegetable or olive oil
¼ cup (55ml) lemon juice
1 teaspoon tamari or sea salt
1 tablespoon freshly chopped or dried herbs of choice (optional)

Put all the ingredients in a screw-top jar and shake it vigorously to combine them. Pour over the salad
Makes ½ cup (150ml).

PEPPERONATA

YOGURT DRESSING

PEPPERONATA

A strongly flavored crunchy salad that you can serve as an antipasto or as a side dish.

INGREDIENTS
½ cup (110ml) olive oil
4 large peppers: red, yellow, green, or orange, or all four together, cut lengthwise into 1in- (2.5cm-) wide strips
½ cup (50g) sliced black Greek or Italian olives
2 tablespoons capers, chopped if large (optional)
sea salt

Heat the oil in a large frying pan or wok. Add the peppers and stir-fry them until they soften. Add the olives and capers, and cook for 2 minutes more. Season with salt to suit your taste.
Serves 4–6.

YOGURT DRESSING

This combination of sweet and sharp goes particularly well with peppers.

INGREDIENTS
¼ cup (55ml) vegetable or olive oil
juice of ½ orange
¼ cup (55ml) yogurt
1½ teaspoons tamari

Blend all the ingredients until smooth.
Makes ½ cup (150ml).

BASIC SALAD DRESSING

HUMMUS-BI-TAHINI

A savory dip that makes a meal in itself when served with fresh vegetable crudités.

INGREDIENTS

1 cup (175g) dried chickpeas
¼ cup (55ml) tahini
½ teaspoon chili powder
1 teaspoon salt
juice of 1 lemon
1 tablespoon olive oil
½ teaspoon paprika
½ teaspoon ground cumin
1 teaspoon chopped parsley

Soak the chickpeas overnight in cold water. Drain and simmer in plenty of fresh water over medium heat until cooked (about 45–60 minutes). Drain off the cooking liquid, reserving a few spoonfuls. When the chickpeas are cool, grind them in a food processor to a smooth, creamy consistency. If the mixture is too stiff, add some of the reserved liquid while blending. Add the tahini, chili powder, salt, and lemon juice, and mix the ingredients together thoroughly. Spoon the hummus into a shallow dish, pour the olive oil on top, and sprinkle with paprika, ground cumin, and chopped parsley. Serve with warm pita bread, olives, crudités, or any salad of your choice. *Makes 1½ cups (450ml).*

WALDORF SALAD

This slight variation on the recipe created at New York's Waldorf-Astoria has a wonderfully crisp texture.

INGREDIENTS

4 apples, cored and diced
juice of 1 lemon
½ cup (50g) walnuts, chopped
2 carrots, finely grated
¾ cup (75g) raisins
2 stalks celery, finely chopped
1 cup (225ml) yogurt, sour cream, or eggless mayonnaise
5 or 6 large lettuce leaves

Combine all the ingredients, except the lettuce, stirring with a fork. Place the mixture in the refrigerator for at least 1 hour, to allow it to set. Serve on a bed of lettuce leaves laid in a bowl or on individual plates. *Serves 4.*

CRUDITÉS

HUMMUS-BI-TAHINI

GUACAMOLE DIP

GUACAMOLE SALAD OR DIP

If you like avocados, you will enjoy this slightly spicy traditional Mexican dish.

INGREDIENTS

1 large avocado
juice of 1 lemon
1½ tablespoons yogurt
¼ teaspoon ground coriander seeds
¼ teaspoon ground cumin
pinch cayenne pepper
sea salt
½ green pepper, finely chopped (optional)

Peel, pit, and roughly chop the avocado. Place in a food processor with the lemon juice, and blend until the mixture is smooth. Add the yogurt, spices, and sea salt, and pulse the processor a few times to mix. Transfer the guacamole to a bowl, and carefully stir in half of the chopped green pepper, if using, reserving the remainder to sprinkle on top of the mixture as decoration. Guacamole can be served as a salad on a bed of tortilla chips, or as a dip for crudités such as celery and carrots. *Makes 1¼ cups (300ml).*

MAIN COURSES

Yogic cooking is meant to be as simple, fresh, and energy-giving as possible. These appetizing recipes are easy to cook at home without resorting to convenience foods. See them as suggestions to be adapted to your own tastes.

UPPAMA

This variation of the traditional South Indian breakfast may be served on its own or with yogurt.

INGREDIENTS

2 cups (250g) coarse semolina
½ cup (110ml) oil
1 large potato, diced
½ teaspoon black mustard seeds
½ teaspoon fennel or cumin seeds
1 teaspoon finely chopped fresh ginger
1 or 2 green chilies, seeded
and finely chopped (optional)
2 tomatoes, roughly chopped
¼ green pepper, finely chopped
½ cup (50g) cabbage, finely chopped
1 carrot, finely chopped
approximately 4 cups (1 liter) freshly boiled water
¼ teaspoon salt
2 tablespoons finely chopped fresh coriander
2 teaspoons ghee or butter

Roast the semolina gently in a dry frying pan for about 3 minutes, stirring it frequently to prevent burning, and then set aside. The semolina should steam and smell slightly smoky. Heat the oil in a large deep frying pan, and deep-fry the diced potato; drain well on paper towels and set aside. Add the mustard seeds and the fennel or cumin seeds to the oil in the frying pan; as soon as they start to crackle and pop, reduce the heat and add the chopped ginger, chilies, and tomatoes. Stir the mixture well and add the remaining vegetables.

  Simmer for 5 minutes. The vegetables should be slightly softened but still firm. Add the water, salt, and chopped coriander, and mix together. Pour the semolina into the frying pan, stirring briskly to prevent lumps from forming. Add the fried potato and the ghee or butter, and mix together. If the mixture seems too dry, add a little more water, but it should not be pasty or too sticky. Remove from the heat and serve immediately.
Serves 4.

RAISIN CHUTNEY

A quick, tasty, and easy-to-make condiment to serve with any vegetable or grain dish.

INGREDIENTS

1 cup (150g) raisins
2 tablespoons hot water
1½ teaspoons chopped fresh ginger
¼ teaspoon cayenne pepper
¼ teaspoon salt
juice of ½ lemon

Soak the raisins in the hot water for 15 minutes. Then place all the ingredients in a blender, adding the lemon juice last. Process until the mixture forms a coarse paste. *Makes ½ cup (150ml).*

CUCUMBER RAITA

There are endless possible variations on this fresh and cooling side dish.

INGREDIENTS

½ cup (150ml) yogurt
1 tablespoon lemon juice
½ teaspoon salt
pinch of cayenne pepper
½–1 teaspoon grated fresh ginger
1 cucumber, grated
pinch ground cumin
2 tablespoons finely chopped fresh cilantro leaves

Mix together the yogurt, lemon juice, salt, cayenne pepper, and ginger. Stir in the cucumber, and then sprinkle the cumin on top. Garnish with cilantro.
Makes 2 cups (400ml).

VARIATIONS: Instead of cucumber, try finely chopped tomato, diced cooked potato, diced and seeded red or green peppers, or even banana.

BIRYANI RICE

This North Indian dish can be served as part of a lavish banquet, or as a simple family meal in its own right.

INGREDIENTS

2 tablespoons ghee or butter
1 green pepper, seeded and chopped
4 whole cloves
4 cardamom pods
2in- (5cm-) stick cinnamon, broken into 3 pieces
1 large tomato, finely chopped
1¼ cups (150g) uncooked basmati rice
2 teaspoons salt
¼ teaspoon cayenne pepper (optional)
½ small eggplant, cubed
2 carrots, diced
1 cup (110g) fresh or frozen peas
1 cup (110g) cauliflower florets
3 cups (725ml) water

Melt the ghee or butter in a large saucepan, and cook the green pepper for 2 minutes, stirring constantly. Add the spices, stir them in, and then cook for a few more minutes. Stir in the tomato, and continue cooking for 5 minutes more. Pour in the rice, and season with salt and cayenne, if using; stir the mixture to coat the rice with sauce. Add the vegetables and the water, stir, and bring to a boil. Cover with a tight-fitting lid and simmer for about 20 minutes. Turn off the heat, and let the rice stand, covered, for 10 minutes. Do not remove the lid from the pan until the full time has elapsed.
Serves 6.

COCONUT CHUTNEY

A tangy condiment that goes well with Uppama, Dosas (see p.136), or any other Indian-style dish.

INGREDIENTS

1 tablespoon oil
¾ teaspoon black mustard seeds
1¼ cups (110g) fresh coconut, grated
½ cup (150ml) water
½ teaspoon crushed dried chilies or fresh green
chili pepper, seeded and chopped
2–3 tablespoons lemon juice
½ teaspoon salt

Heat the oil in a pan with a lid. Add the mustard seeds, and roast until they start to crackle and pop, being careful not to burn them. Remove the pan from the heat, and set aside. Put the coconut, water, and crushed chilies or chopped green chili pepper in a blender, and process until the mixture is smooth, adding more water if necessary. Transfer the mixture to a bowl and stir in the mustard seeds, oil, lemon juice, and salt.
Makes 2 cups (400ml).

RAISIN CHUTNEY

CUCUMBER RAITA

BIRYANI RICE

COCONUT CHUTNEY

INDIAN DHAL

*A protein-packed meal that is meant to be
served over rice, dhal is a staple dish
throughout the Indian subcontinent.*

INGREDIENTS

*1 cup (175g) red lentils, yellow or green split peas,
or split yellow mung beans
3 cups (725ml) water
2 tablespoons oil
½ teaspoon black mustard seeds
1 teaspoon cumin seeds
1 tablespoon hot green chilies,
chopped and seeded (optional)
4 whole cloves
1 teaspoon salt
½ teaspoon turmeric*

Cook the lentils, split peas, or mung beans in water until
mushy (20–30 minutes). Meanwhile, heat the oil in a
frying pan and add the mustard seeds. When these begin
to pop, add the cumin seeds and sauté briefly, being
careful not to let them burn. Add the chopped chilies
(if using), cloves, salt, and turmeric to the frying pan, and
continue frying for a few minutes. Add the fried spice
mixture to the lentils, peas, or mung beans. Stir well, and
reheat gently but thoroughly.
Serves 4–6.

VARIATIONS: Add a selection of diced vegetables, such as
zucchini, tomatoes, green peppers, or a combination of
these while the lentils are cooking.
If you like, add some finely chopped fresh cilantro leaves
at the end of the cooking time, just before serving. Some
people prefer very thin dhal; if this mixture is too thick,
add water to achieve the desired consistency, stir to
combine, and then reheat thoroughly.

DOSAS

*Serve Dosas hot with Coconut Chutney (see p.135)
or filled with Curried Vegetables (see below).*

INGREDIENTS

*1¼ cups (225g) brown or basmati rice
½ cup (75g) urid dhal (lentil-like beans
available from Indian food stores)
few fenugreek seeds (optional)
salt, water, oil*

Soak the rice and urid dhal, and fenugreek seeds if using,
overnight in plenty of water. Drain off most of the water
and grind the mixture in a blender to a smooth, slightly
gritty paste. Add salt and enough water to form a thin
batter. Let the batter stand at room temperature for about
24 hours, to allow the dosa flavor to develop.

Heat a nonstick frying pan, and lightly oil the surface.
Pour some batter into the center of the pan. Press gently
with the back of a spoon to spread outward, forming a
large thin pancake. Sprinkle the surface of the pancake
with oil as it becomes firm. When the underside is crisp
and golden, turn and cook other side.
Makes 4–5 pancakes.

CURRIED VEGETABLES

*This is a basic recipe, which can be adapted
to make use of vegetables in season.*

INGREDIENTS

*2 tablespoons oil
1 teaspoon black mustard seeds
1 tomato, chopped
¼ teaspoon turmeric
1 teaspoon curry powder
1 teaspoon salt
1 cauliflower, separated into florets
2 potatoes, cubed and parboiled
¼ cup (55ml) water
lemon juice to taste*

Heat the oil in a large pan. Add the mustard seeds, cover,
and cook until they pop. Reduce the heat and add the
tomato. Cook, covered, until soft (3–4 minutes). Add the
turmeric, curry powder, and salt, and then the cauliflower
florets, stirring them gently to coat them with spices. Add
the potatoes, water, and lemon juice. Continue cooking
over medium heat, covered. Stir gently until the potatoes
and cauliflower are just tender (about 15–20 minutes),
adding more water if necessary.
Serves 6.

VEGETABLE LASAGNE

*A well-known and ever-popular dish;
vegans can leave out the cheese.*

INGREDIENTS

*6 cups (175g) spinach, steamed and squeezed dry
10oz (284g) block firm tofu, crumbled and drained
salt and freshly ground black pepper
2 medium zucchini, cut into julienne strips
1 medium red pepper, cut into julienne strips
olive oil
4 cups (1kg) Tomato Sauce (see p.143)
6 sheets dried lasagne noodles, cooked and drained
1 cup (120g) grated vegetarian Cheddar cheese (optional)
2 tablespoons vegetarian Parmesan cheese or yeast (optional)
2 tablespoons sunflower or sesame seeds*

Chop the spinach, mix with the tofu, and season with salt and pepper. Sauté the zucchini and pepper in the oil for 3 minutes. Preheat the oven to 350°F/180°C. Put a layer of tomato sauce in an oiled 10 x 8in (20 x 25cm) baking dish. Cover this with a layer of lasagne noodles, half the tofu/spinach mixture, then half the zucchini and peppers. Sprinkle with half the grated cheese (if using). Repeat the layers, and top with vegetarian Parmesan cheese or yeast (if using), and sunflower or sesame seeds. Bake for 50–60 minutes until bubbling and golden.
Serves 4.

GREEK VEGETABLES

*Serve with simply cooked rice or pasta, thick
slices of fresh bread, and a typical Greek salad.*

INGREDIENTS

*3 tablespoons olive oil
10 small new potatoes, scrubbed
4 medium zucchini, cut into 2in- (5cm-) julienne strips
4 medium tomatoes, chopped
2 tablespoons chopped fresh dill, or 2 teaspoons dried dill
2¼ cups (600 ml) water
salt and pepper*

Heat the oil in a heavy, lidded pan. Sauté the potatoes until they begin to soften, stirring occasionally. Add the zucchini, tomatoes, and dill. Barely cover the vegetables with cold water, bring to a boil, cover, and simmer until soft (about 25–30 minutes), stirring gently. Add a little more water if necessary. Add salt and pepper to taste. Serve with rice or pasta, fresh bread, and a salad of lettuce, cucumber, tomatoes, calamata olives, and feta cheese.
Serves 6.

*VEGETABLE
LASAGNE*

PASTA ALLA POMODORO

*A simple and speedy dish that tastes
quite exotic and extremely good.*

INGREDIENTS

*2 tablespoons olive oil
½ teaspoon dried hot pepper flakes
1 large red pepper, sliced lengthwise into
½in- (1.5cm-) strips
28oz (800g) canned plum tomatoes
2 tablespoons tomato purée
1 cup (175g) Greek or Italian black olives
2 tablespoons Spanish capers
salt and freshly ground black pepper
18oz (500g) penne or rigatoni*

Heat the oil in a saucepan or deep frying pan. Add the hot pepper flakes, and cook for few seconds, stirring to prevent them from burning. Add the strips of red pepper and cook gently, covered, for about 10 minutes, until they start to soften. Add the tomatoes, breaking them up with a wooden spoon, and stir in the tomato purée. Bring to a boil, lower the heat, and simmer, uncovered, for about 30 minutes, stirring occasionally. Add the olives and capers, and cook for 5 minutes more. Season to taste with salt and pepper. Meanwhile, cook the pasta in boiling, salted water until *al dente*. Drain the pasta and serve immediately with the sauce.
Serves 6.

STUFFED CABBAGE

These flavorsome bundles of beans and brown rice are seasoned with caraway and served with Tomato Sauce.

INGREDIENTS
1 large Savoy cabbage
1 teaspoon caraway seeds
1 tablespoon olive oil or butter
½ cup (75g) cooked rice
2 tablespoons raisins (optional)
1 cup (200g) cooked lima or other beans
salt and pepper
1½ cup (500g) Tomato Sauce (see p.143)

Preheat the oven to 350°F/180°C. Remove six large outer leaves from the cabbage. Rinse the leaves, then steam until just wilted (about 3–4 minutes). Shred quarter of the remaining cabbage, saving the rest for another recipe. Sauté the shredded cabbage with the caraway seeds in olive oil or butter for 10 minutes. Remove from the heat and add the cooked rice, raisins (if using), and the cooked lima or other beans. Season to taste.

Place a spoonful of the rice mixture on each cabbage leaf. Roll up each leaf, enclosing the filling, fold in the ends of each roll, and secure firmly with a toothpick. Place the bundles close together in a lightly oiled baking dish. Cover with the Tomato Sauce and bake for 30 minutes. *Serves 6.*

CHESTNUT ROAST

This rich and warming festive dish is ideal for celebrations, perhaps served with roast parsnips, brussels sprouts, and a sauce.

INGREDIENTS
1 cup (175g) shelled chestnuts
1 cup (175g) millet
1¼ cups (150g) mixed nuts: e.g., almonds, brazil nuts, and peanuts
½ cup (150ml) oil
2 small carrots, grated
½ small cabbage, finely sliced
2 small sticks celery, sliced
½ bunch broccoli, broken into florets
1 tablespoon finely chopped fresh mixed herbs
2 tablespoons tomato purée
2 tablespoons tahini
black pepper
salt or tamari to taste
1 tablespoon sliced almonds
1 tablespoon pumpkin seeds

Boil the chestnuts until tender. Drain the water off and reserve it to use as stock. Bring a large pan of cold water to the boil. Add the millet and simmer for 10–15 minutes until tender. Grind the mixed nuts to the consistency of coarse breadcrumbs, and then roast in the oven at 400°F/200°C for 10 minutes, stirring once halfway through the roasting. Reduce the temperature of the oven to 350°F/180°C.

Heat the oil in a large pan; add the grated carrots, sliced cabbage, and celery sticks, and cook gently, covered, for 10 minutes. When the vegetables are nearly cooked, add the broccoli florets and cook until they are tender (about 10 minutes). Add the mixed herbs, tomato purée, tahini, boiled chestnuts, cooked millet, roasted nuts, and black pepper, stirring the mixture thoroughly to ensure that the ingredients are well combined. Season with salt or tamari. Spoon the mixture, in batches, into the bowl of a food processor, and process until the ingredients are roughly chopped and sticky. Place the mixture in a large loaf pan, and garnish the top with the sliced almonds and pumpkin seeds. Bake for 35–40 minutes.

Chestnut Roast can be served with Miso-almond Sauce or Tomato Sauce (see p.143), using the reserved chestnut cooking water as stock. *Serves 6.*

STUFFED CABBAGE

SHEPHERD'S PIE

A hearty mix of beans and vegetables, baked with a crusty brown topping, makes an interesting vegetarian variation on the traditional dish.

INGREDIENTS
1½ cups (225g) adzuki beans
1½ cups (225g) green lentils, rinsed
2 tablespoons oil
2 carrots, grated
¼ large red cabbage, finely chopped or grated
1 teaspoon ground cumin
1 teaspoon ground cinnamon
1 tablespoon freshly chopped thyme
½ teaspoon freshly grated nutmeg
2 parsnips, diced
½ head of broccoli, cut into small florets
¼ cauliflower, cut into small florets
4 tablespoons tomato purée
14oz (400g) canned tomatoes, chopped or blended
salt and pepper
about ½ cup (125m) apple juice concentrate

TOPPING
1 small rutabaga, cubed
3 medium potatoes, cubed
1 parsnip, cubed
1 tablespoon margarine or butter
1–2 tablespoons soy milk
2 tablespoons finely chopped fresh parsley
1–2 tablespoons tahini

Soak the adzuki beans overnight in plenty of cold water. Drain and place in a large pan with the lentils and at least twice their volume of cold water. Boil hard for 10 minutes. Reduce the heat to simmer, cover, and cook for 20 minutes more until tender. Drain.

Heat the oil in a large pan; add the grated carrots, cabbage, spices, and herbs. Cook, stirring frequently, for 5 minutes. Add the parsnips and cook for 5 minutes; then add the broccoli, cauliflower, tomato purée, and tomatoes, and season with salt and pepper to suit your taste. Cook for 5 minutes. Add the beans, lentils, and apple juice. The mixture should be soft, but not runny.

To make the topping, boil the cubed rutabaga, potatoes, and parsnip until tender; drain and mash them together with margarine or butter and soy milk. Add the chopped parsley and the tahini, and stir them into the mashed vegetables. Pour the lentil and vegetable mixture into an oiled baking dish and cover with the topping mixture. Bake at 375°F/190°C for 35–40 minutes until the topping is crunchy and golden.
Serves 6.

POTATO AND ZUCCHINI CASSEROLE

This dish of creamy zucchini with a cheesy potato crust is delicious with whole-grain bread.

INGREDIENTS
2 tablespoons sunflower seeds
½ teaspoon tamari
1½lb (700g) potatoes, peeled and diced
3 large zucchini, scrubbed and sliced
2 tablespoons chopped fresh basil
3 tablespoons milk
1 tablespoon butter
salt and pepper
½ cup (75g) grated vegetarian Cheddar cheese
½ teaspoon paprika

Preheat the oven to 350°F/180°C. Toast the sunflower seeds for 5 minutes, then toss with tamari. Meanwhile boil the potatoes until soft; drain well and set aside. Lightly steam the zucchini, and then place them in an oiled baking dish. Sprinkle the zucchini with the sunflower seeds and chopped basil.

Mash the potatoes with milk, butter, and salt and pepper to taste. Spoon the mashed potatoes over the zucchini in the baking dish. Sprinkle with the grated Cheddar cheese and paprika. Bake for 25–30 minutes until the cheese is golden and bubbling.
Serves 4–6.

COOKING PEAS, BEANS, AND LENTILS

Peas, beans, and lentils provide an important source of nutrition in a vegetarian diet. Dried peas and beans need soaking in water before being cooked. You can speed up the soaking process by bringing them to a boil and then letting them stand. The water should be discarded. Cook peas, beans, and lentils by simmering in a large, covered pan until they are tender, stirring to prevent sticking.

CHILI CON VEGGIES

A spicy and delicious dish that is amazingly simple and quick to prepare with canned beans.

INGREDIENTS
*1 cup (200g) dried red kidney beans
(or canned beans)
1½ teaspoons chili powder
½ teaspoon ground cumin
½ teaspoon turmeric
1 tablespoon tamari
4 tablespoons vegetable oil
1 large green pepper, seeded and chopped
3 celery ribs, chopped
1 large carrot, chopped
2 large tomatoes, chopped
4 tablespoons tomato paste
3 tablespoons lemon juice
large pinch salt*

Soak the kidney beans overnight in cold water. Drain off the water, transfer the beans to a pan, and cover with fresh water. Bring to a boil, and boil for 10 minutes. Reduce the heat, cover, and simmer gently for 30 minutes more until tender. Drain and set aside.

Briefly sauté the spices in oil, stirring to avoid burning, then add the green pepper, celery, and carrot, and cook for a few more minutes. Add the remaining ingredients and stir well. Simmer for 15 minutes, add the cooked red kidney beans, and simmer for 15 minutes more. Serve with corn bread.
Serves 4.

GRAIN KNOW-HOW

▶ Grains are one of the most important elements in a vegetarian diet, supplying about half the amino acids necessary to form protein. They are also inexpensive, easy to prepare, and convenient to store. A wide variety of grains, including wheat berries, brown rice, millet, buckwheat, bulgur, oats, and corn, is available.

▶ Grains are easy to prepare. Begin by rinsing them in several changes of cold water, until the water runs clear. Drain, and place in a heavy pan with four times their volume of water. Bring to a boil, and add a dash of salt if desired. Stir once, cover the pan, reduce the heat to its lowest setting, and simmer until all the water is absorbed.

▶ To give grains a sweeter, nuttier flavor, dry-roast them first in the oven at 350°F/175°C until golden brown. Another variation is to cook the grain in vegetable stock, or juice, instead of water.

SIMPLE BEAN LOAF

This is a good way to use leftover grains and beans, and can be served with Tomato Sauce or Gado Gado peanut sauce (see p.143).

INGREDIENTS
*1 cup (175g) cooked pinto or lima beans
4 cups (450g) cooked brown rice
1 cup (110g) whole-wheat breadcrumbs or wheat germ
1 cup (110g) rolled oats
1 cup (110g) chopped nuts (optional)
¼ cup (55ml) oil
1 tablespoon chopped parsley
1 tablespoon basil
½ tablespoon thyme
tamari*

Preheat the oven to 350°F/175°C. Mash the pinto or lima beans with the back of a fork, and then mix them well with the brown rice, breadcrumbs or wheat germ, rolled oats, chopped nuts (if using), oil, parsley, basil, thyme, and tamari to taste. Transfer to a large lightly oiled loaf pan and bake for 1 hour.
Serves 6.

BULGUR WITH VEGETABLES

Colorful vegetables, lightly cooked with cracked wheat, make a satisfying and wholesome dish.

INGREDIENTS
*1 cup (175g) bulgur (cracked wheat)
4 tablespoons butter
1lb (450g) mixed vegetables, chopped into bite-sized pieces,
e.g., carrot, celery, green beans, green or
red pepper, zucchini, broccoli
1¾ cups (425ml) water
2 tablespoons tamari
2 tablespoons chopped basil leaves*

Sauté the bulgur in half the butter until it is golden brown. Add the mixed vegetables, water, tamari, and chopped basil leaves. Stir well and cover. Simmer gently for 20 minutes, stirring occasionally to prevent the mixture sticking, until all the liquid has been absorbed and the vegetables are just tender. Add the remaining butter, mix gently, and serve.
Serves 4–6.

MUNG BEAN CURRY

*A typical, simple Indian dish, made with
the most easily digested of beans.*

INGREDIENTS
*1¼ cups (225g) whole mung beans
3 cups (725ml) cold water
pinch turmeric
4 small or 2 large tomatoes, roughly chopped
1in- (3cm-) piece fresh ginger, peeled and
finely chopped
5 or 6 large spinach leaves, finely chopped
½ teaspoon ground coriander
and/or ground cumin seeds
1 tablespoon ghee
1 teaspoon mustard and/or fennel seeds
salt*

Wash the mung beans and drain thoroughly.
Dry-roast in a frying pan over a medium flame
until the beans are dry and give off a toasted aroma.
Transfer to a large saucepan and add the water and
turmeric. Bring to a boil and simmer for 15 minutes.
Add the tomatoes and ginger, and cook for 10 minutes
more until the beans are tender. Add the spinach, ground
coriander seeds and/or ground cumin seeds. Stir well and
cover. Melt the ghee in a frying pan and, when it is hot,
add the mustard and/or fennel seeds; roast until the seeds
pop, and then add to the mung beans and stir well.
Season with salt to taste and serve.
Serves 4.

STEAMED VEGETABLES

*The vegetables, cut into attractive shapes and cooked
immediately, retain their fresh, crisp texture.*

INGREDIENTS
*2lb (1kg) assorted vegetables,
e.g., cauliflower, broccoli,
bok choy, Brussels sprouts, zucchini,
and snow peas*

Wash and cut the vegetables into bite-sized pieces. Place
in the top of a steamer, if you have one. Otherwise, place
in a tightly lidded saucepan, with 1 inch (2.5cm) of water.
Put those vegetables that require the longest cooking time
in first, and place the softer ones on top. Place the pan
over a high heat until the water boils, then turn down the
heat and cook, covered, for 8–15 minutes, until the
vegetables are tender but firm. Drain if necessary.
Serves 4.

*STIR-FRIED
VEGETABLES*

STIR-FRIED VEGETABLES

*Made with perfectly fresh vegetables,
this is delicious at any time, whether served alone
or with a sauce of your choice.*

INGREDIENTS
*3 tablespoons vegetable oil
1 carrot, thinly sliced
1 parsnip, thinly sliced
¼ cabbage, finely shredded
1 stick celery, thinly sliced
1 green pepper, thinly sliced
1 red pepper, thinly sliced
¼ bunch broccoli, cut into florets
¼ cauliflower, cut into florets
1 small zucchini, cut into julienne strips*

Heat the oil in a wok or a large frying pan until very hot.
Add the sliced carrots and parsnip, and stir-fry for about
1 minute. Add the shredded cabbage and sliced celery, and
stir-fry for a minute more. Add the remaining vegetables
and stir-fry for another 2–3 minutes. Make sure that the
vegetables are not overcooked. Serve with Tamari Ginger
Sauce (see p.143) and plain boiled rice.
Serves 4–6.

SAUCES & CONDIMENTS

Even the simplest meal can become something special when served
with an appetizing sauce. Condiments add flavor and nutrition,
as well as aiding digestion. A little usually goes a long way!

TACO SAUCE

*A great way to spice up any dish. Try it with the
Simple Bean Loaf (see p.140) or organic corn chips.*

INGREDIENTS

*1 large tomato, chopped
2 tablespoons tomato paste
½ tablespoon lemon juice
⅛ teaspoon mustard powder
⅛ teaspoon cinnamon powder
¼ teaspoon cumin powder
salt, black pepper, and cayenne pepper to taste*

Combine all the ingredients in a bowl and mix them
together thoroughly. Serve immediately.
Makes about 1 cup (240g).

PUMPKIN SEED WAKAME

*Sprinkle these savory seeds over soups
and salads as a condiment.*

INGREDIENTS

*¼ cup (25g) pumpkin seeds, rinsed
1 teaspoon dried wakame seaweed flakes*

Dry-roast the pumpkin seeds with the wakame in a frying
pan until the seeds pop. Grind together in a food
processor to the consistency of coarse breadcrumbs.
Makes ¼ cup (25g).

SHOYU SUNFLOWER SEEDS

*These make a delicious snack by themselves,
and can be served with salads or grain dishes.*

INGREDIENTS

*¼ cup (25g) sunflower seeds, rinsed
½–1 teaspoon shoyu*

Dry-roast the sunflower seeds in a frying pan until they
are golden and slightly puffy. Remove from the heat, and
add enough shoyu to coat all the seeds.
Makes ¼ cup (25g).

GOMASHIO

*A typical Japanese macrobiotic condiment
that is both appetizing and highly nutritious.*

INGREDIENTS

*¼ cup (25g) sesame seeds, rinsed and drained
½ teaspoon unrefined sea or rock salt*

Roast the seeds in a hot oven for 10 minutes, stirring
once. Add the salt and roast for another minute.
Cool slightly, then grind with a pestle and mortar.
Makes ¼ cup (25g).

SHOYU SUNFLOWER SEEDS

PUMPKIN SEED WAKAME

TACO SAUCE

GOMASHIO

TOMATO SAUCE

If you prefer a smoother tomato sauce to pour over a dish or for use in other recipes, such as Vegetable Lasagne (see p.137), purée in a blender.

INGREDIENTS

2 tablespoons olive oil
1lb (450g) mixed diced vegetables,
e.g., zucchini, green pepper, and carrot
1 bay leaf
1 teaspoon dried oregano
½ teaspoon dried thyme
¼ teaspoon dried basil
1 teaspoon salt
480g (1lb) fresh tomatoes, roughly chopped
28oz (800g) canned tomatoes
3 tablespoons tomato paste
¼ teaspoon honey
⅛ teaspoon pepper

Heat the oil in a pan over a medium heat; sauté the vegetables for a few minutes, stirring well. Add the herbs and cook for few more minutes, stirring. Add the other ingredients and simmer for a further 45 minutes. Leave the sauce to stand for as long as possible before serving, to bring out the full flavor.
Makes about 4 cups (1kg).

MISO-ALMOND SAUCE

INGREDIENTS

4 tablespoons light miso
6 tablespoons almond butter
¾ cup (175ml) boiling water

Put the miso, almond butter, and half the boiling water in a bowl. Mash the mixture thoroughly with a spoon until it forms a smooth paste. Gradually add the remaining water and mix until well combined.
Makes 1½ cups (375ml).

TAMARI-GINGER SAUCE

INGREDIENTS

3 tablespoons tamari
3 tablespoons water
3 teaspoons fresh grated ginger

Mix all the ingredients together. Leave to stand for at least 2 hours to allow the flavor to develop.
Makes ½ cup (150ml).

TOMATO SAUCE

TOMATO SAUCE

GADO GADO

Be sure to use fresh, unprocessed peanut butter for this rich Indonesian peanut sauce.

INGREDIENTS

1½ tablespoons vegetable oil
½ large celery rib or ¼ green pepper, diced
1 tablespoon chopped or grated fresh ginger
curry powder, cumin powder, or
cayenne pepper to taste (optional)
1 cup (150g) natural peanut butter
1¼ cups (300ml) boiling water
⅔ cup (50g) dry unsweetened coconut
2 tablespoons tamari or shoyu
1½ teaspoons honey
juice of ½ lemon

Heat the oil in a wok. Add the diced celery or diced green pepper, ginger, and curry powder, cumin, or cayenne pepper (if using), and sauté over a low heat until soft. Add the peanut butter, stirring to prevent it from scorching. When the mixture is bubbling, stir in enough boiling water to give it the consistency of thin cream.

Turn the heat up high, bring the mixture to a boil, then lower the heat and simmer. Add the dry shredded coconut, tamari or shoyu, honey, and lemon juice, and stir the ingredients together thoroughly. Taste and adjust the seasonings: the flavor should be slightly tart. Continue simmering the mixture until the oil rises to top of the sauce (about 10 minutes).

Gado Gado will add piquance to the simplest of dishes and is ideal to serve with a selection of lightly steamed vegetables, such as carrots, green beans or snow peas, asparagus, broccoli, and cauliflower.
Makes 1½ cups (450 ml).

DESSERTS

Even the staunchest vegetarian can have a sweet tooth, but this can be satisfied in a natural, healthy way, rather than with empty calories. Desserts can be as simple or as eleborate as your schedule permits.

STUFFED BAKED APPLES

A delicious, warming winter dessert that can be baked in the oven along with the main course.

INGREDIENTS

6 large apples
⅓ cup (50g) raisins and/or chopped dates
½ cup (50g) chopped walnuts or sesame seeds
¼ cup (60ml) apple juice
yogurt to serve (optional)

Preheat oven to 350°F/180°C. Core, but do not peel, the apples. Place them on a baking sheet. Combine the raisins and/or dates, walnuts or sesame seeds, and apple juice. Fill the cored center of each apple with some of the raisin mixture, until the mixture is used up. Bake the apples in the oven for about 50 minutes, but do not overcook. Serve hot, with yogurt if you wish.
Serves 6.

CHEESECAKE

This rich and easily prepared dish is ideal for special occasions.

INGREDIENTS

1¼ cups (110g) crushed graham crackers
¾ cup (75g) coarsely chopped walnuts
4 tablespoons melted butter
14oz (400g) cream cheese
1 cup (275ml) yogurt
3–4 tablespoons honey
1 teaspoon vanilla extract
fresh fruit for garnish

Mix together the crushed graham crackers, chopped walnuts, and butter, and press into a 9 inch- (23cm-) springform pan. Chill in the refrigerator until the mixture sets or, for a crisper texture, bake in the oven at 350°F/180°C for about 10 minutes, until it turns golden brown, and then set aside to cool.

Beat the cream cheese and the yogurt together until smooth. If possible, use an electric mixer so that the mixture becomes light and airy. Add the honey and vanilla extract. Pour over the crust and chill until firm. Just before serving the cheesecake, decorate the top with attractively sliced fresh fruit.
Serves 6–8.

VARIATIONS: To make a Chocolate Cheesecake, add ¼ cup (25g) of cocoa powder to the cream cheese filling and, before serving, decorate the top with dark chocolate curls or grated chocolate. Be careful not to overdo it, or the result will be too rich.

For Orange or Lemon Cheesecake, add 2 tablespoons of orange or lemon juice, and 2 teaspoons of finely grated orange or lemon zest to the cream cheese mixture, and decorate the top with small pieces of fresh citrus fruit.

CHEESECAKE

FRAISES SUPREME

A light summer delight that can be adapted by substituting almost any juicy fruit for the strawberries.

INGREDIENTS

*4 tablespoons agar agar flakes or other
vegetarian gelling powder
1¼ cups (300ml) cold water
1¼ cups (300ml) hot water
½ cup (150ml) honey
1¼ cups (300ml) orange juice
2 tablespoons lemon juice
3–4 sliced strawberries
whipped cream and 6 whole strawberries
for garnish*

Mix the agar agar flakes, or other gelling agent, with cold water in a saucepan. Leave to soften for 1 minute, and then add the hot water. Bring to the boil, and boil for 2 minutes. Leave to cool slightly, then add the honey, orange juice, and lemon juice. Add the sliced strawberries, and stir gently. Pour into individual serving bowls and leave to set in a refrigerator for about 2 hours. Garnish each serving with whipped cream and a strawberry. *Serves 6.*

VARIATION: Instead of strawberries, use sliced bananas, grapes, or other fruits or berries in season.

BURFI

*A traditional Indian milk pudding,
often served on festive occasions.*

INGREDIENTS

*1 cup (285ml) honey
1 cup (240g) butter
¼ teaspoon ground cardamom
¼ cup (55ml) milk
1 cup (110g) ground nuts,
e.g., almonds, walnuts, or pistachios
1¼ cups (275g) powdered milk*

In a saucepan, heat the honey, butter, ground cardamom, and milk over low heat, stirring to avoid burning, until well blended. Add the ground nuts and stir to combine, then remove the pan from the heat. Add the powdered milk slowly, stirring until completely dissolved. The mixture will gradually thicken. When it is very stiff, spread in a shallow pan and place in the refrigerator to set. Cut into diamond shapes, and serve at room temperature. *Makes 30–36 squares.*

TOFU CREAM PIE

*This is the perfect nondairy creamy dessert
– and it is surprisingly healthy!*

CRUST

*¼ cup (55ml) maple syrup
¼ cup (55ml) light vegetable oil
¼ cup (55ml) water
1¼ cups (150g) rolled oats
½ cup (50g) plain whole-wheat flour
¼ cup (55ml) sunflower seeds
pinch salt*

FILLING:

*1½ lb (720g) soft tofu
1–2 tablespoons tahini
grated rind of 1 lemon
½ cup (110ml) maple syrup
¼ cup (55ml) light vegetable oil
¼ cup (55ml) water
pinch salt
fresh fruit for garnish*

Preheat the oven to 400°F/200°C. Lightly oil a 9in- (23cm-) springform pan. To make the crust, whisk together the maple syrup, vegetable oil, and water in a bowl, and then combine with the rolled oats, whole-wheat flour, sunflower seeds, and salt. Pat the mixture into the pan, pushing some crumbs up the sides to form a rim about 1in (2.5cm) deep.

Bake the crust for 10–15 minutes until golden brown. Place the pan on a wire rack and leave to cool. Reduce the oven temperature to 350°F/180°C.

To make the filling, combine the tofu, tahini, lemon rind, maple syrup, vegetable oil, water, and salt in a food processor, and process until smooth. Pour the filling into the prebaked crust, and bake in the oven for 30 minutes, until the filling is golden and set.

Serve in thin slices, garnished with strawberries, blueberries, or the fruit of your choice. *Serves 8.*

BREAD & MUFFINS

Home-baked bread and muffins are irresistible, and generally much healthier than the store-bought varieties. If you can't grind your own flour, buy the freshest stone-ground whole-wheat flour you can find. Most baked goods freeze well.

SAVORY CHEESE MUFFINS

RAISIN-BRAN MUFFINS

These are especially good straight from the oven for breakfast – for variety, try replacing half the brown sugar with molasses.

INGREDIENTS

5 cups (600g) plain whole-wheat flour
1 cup (100g) bran
⅔ cup (150g) raisins
¾ teaspoon salt
2 teaspoons baking powder
6 tablespoons brown sugar
2 cups (½ liter) water
6 tablespoons oil

Preheat the oven to 190°F/375°C. Lightly oil the muffin tin. In a large bowl, mix the whole-wheat flour, bran, raisins, salt, baking powder, and brown sugar together. In another large bowl, combine the water and oil. Add the dry mixture to the water and oil mixture, and fold them together quickly until the dry ingredients are evenly mixed and just moistened. Do not overmix, as this will make the muffins heavier.

Spoon the mixture into the oiled muffin tins, and bake for 20–30 minutes, or until a skewer inserted in the center of a muffin comes out clean. Let the muffins cool slightly in the tin before removing, but serve while still warm for that fresh-baked flavor.
Makes 12 muffins.

SAVORY CHEESE MUFFINS

These unusual savory muffins are a treat with any soup at lunchtime.

INGREDIENTS

¾ cup (100g) grated carrot
5 cups (600g) plain whole-wheat flour
¾ cup (100g) corn kernels
¾ cup (100g) finely chopped zucchini
1¼ cups (150g) grated vegetarian Cheddar cheese
2 teaspoons dried basil
1 teaspoon dried oregano
1 teaspoon baking powder
1 teaspoon salt
black pepper to taste
1 teaspoon brown sugar
28oz (800g) canned tomatoes or 1lb (500g) fresh tomatoes, liquidized or mashed
1 cup (200ml) water
4 tablespoons oil

TOPPING:

1 cup (100g) grated vegetarian Cheddar cheese
1–2 teaspoons dried oregano

Preheat the oven to 375°F/190°C. Lightly oil your muffin tins. In a bowl, mix the grated carrot with the flour, corn, zucchini, cheese, basil, oregano, baking powder, salt, black pepper, and sugar. In another bowl, mix the tomatoes, water, and oil together. Add the dry ingredients to the wet ingredients, and fold together until they are evenly mixed and just moistened.

Spoon the mixture into the oiled muffin tins. Combine the remaining grated cheese and the oregano, and sprinkle over the top of the muffins. Bake for 30 minutes, or until a skewer inserted in the center of a muffin comes out clean.
Makes 20–24 muffins.

VARIATIONS: Try adding fresh rosemary or thyme for another delicious flavor.

Vegans can use soy cheese instead of Cheddar.

WHOLE-WHEAT BREAD

Bread baking is an old skill, and still a very useful one – even imperfect results can be delicious.

INGREDIENTS

2 teaspoons active dried yeast
about 1½ cups (360ml) lukewarm water or milk
2½ tablespoons honey
2 teaspoons sea salt
4 cups (480g) plain whole-wheat flour, plus extra for dusting
2 tablespoons (30ml) vegetable oil

Oil one large loaf pan or two small loaf pans. Sprinkle the yeast onto ½ cup (90ml) of the warm water or milk, add the honey, and leave in a warm place for 10 minutes until the mixture begins to froth. Mix the salt with the flour in a large bowl. Make a well in the center and add the yeast liquid and the oil. With a wooden spoon, gradually incorporate flour from the sides of the well into the liquid, adding more liquid as you work. As the dough stiffens, mix it with the hands until smooth. Transfer the dough to a work surface, and knead thoroughly. Cover, and allow to rise until it has doubled in size (about 1 hour).

Knead the dough again, and divide in two if making two small loaves. Stretch the dough into an oblong roughly the size of the pan, and fit into the pan, pressing down around the edges to give a rounded surface. Sprinkle with the extra flour, cover with a damp dish towel, and leave to rise in a warm place for 30–40 minutes until the dough has risen nearly to the top of the pan.

Preheat the oven to 400°F/200°C. Bake the bread for 45 minutes for one large loaf or 35 minutes for the smaller size. To check if the loaf is done, remove from the pan and tap the bottom; it should sound hollow. If necessary, return to the oven for 5–10 more minutes.
Makes 1 large or 2 small loaves.

VARIATIONS: Try some of these alternatives to vary the flavor.

For a richer flavor, try using different liquids, such as vegetable stock, in the mixture.

To make Poppy Seed Bread, add ½ cup (50g) of poppy seeds, 1 teaspoon of almond extract, and an extra tablespoonful of honey.

For a seed or fruit loaf, add ½ cup (50g) of sunflower or sesame seeds, or ¾ cup (75g) of raisins or dates to the flour.

CORN BREAD

A fast and tempting cross between a bread and a cake – remember that corn bread tends to be slightly crumbly.

INGREDIENTS

4 cups (450g) cornmeal
2½ cups (275g) plain whole-wheat flour
2 cups (50g) bran flakes, crushed
1½ teaspoons baking powder
1½ teaspoons baking soda
¾ teaspoon salt
1 cup (225ml) oil
¼ cup (55ml) honey
2 cups (500ml) milk or water

Preheat the oven to 400°F/200°C. Oil two large loaf pans. Mix the cornmeal, whole-wheat flour, bran flakes, baking powder, baking soda, and salt in a bowl. In another bowl, mix the oil, honey, and milk (or water). Mix the dry ingredients into the oil and milk. You should be able to pour this mixture; if it is too thick, add more milk until you achieve the desired consistency. Pour the mixture into the oiled loaf pans, and bake for 10 minutes. Lower the heat to 325°F/160°C and bake for 40 minutes more until the loaves are risen and golden.
Makes 2 large loaves.

VARIATION: You can use this mixture to make muffins. Preheat the oven to 400°F/200°C. Lightly oil large muffin tins and fill each about two-thirds full with the mixture. Bake for 10 minutes, and then reduce the temperature to 325°F/170°C. Cook for a further 20–30 minutes until the muffins are risen and golden. Cool slightly, and then turn out onto a wire rack.
Makes 24 muffins.

WHOLE-WHEAT BREAD

CAKES & COOKIES

A healthy vegetarian diet doesn't have to be uninteresting, even if it is simple.
There are many natural ingredients readily available to create endless variations.
Use these recipes as a starting point for your own creations.

SIVANANDA COOKIES

*These extra large energy-packed cookies are a staple
after-class treat at Sivananda Yoga Centers.*

INGREDIENTS
*2 cups (250g) oats
1 cup (110g) plain whole-wheat flour
⅓ cup (50g) raisins
½ cup (50g) raw unsalted peanuts
1 cup (150g) brown sugar
1½ teaspoons ground cinnamon
½ teaspoon ground nutmeg
1½ teaspoons ground ginger
½ teaspoon baking powder
pinch salt
¾ cup (200ml) sunflower oil
1 cup (200ml) milk or water*

Preheat the oven to 400°F/200°C. Mix the dry ingredients
in a large bowl; add the oil and mix well. Stir in enough
milk or water to make a firm mixture. Place heaped
spoonfuls on an oiled baking tray, and flatten them into
4in (10cm) rounds. Bake for 12–15 minutes until golden
at the edges. Cool on a rack.

These highly nutritious cookies are hard to resist, and
really do make a meal in themselves.
Makes 12 cookies.

CARROT CAKE

*An attractive and appetizing way to encourage
your children to eat vegetables.*

INGREDIENTS
*1 cup (225ml) oil
1 cup (125g) brown sugar
½ cup (110ml) honey
1½ cups (325ml) soy milk
6 cups (700g) plain whole-wheat flour
2 teaspoons baking powder
1 teaspoon salt
1½ teaspoons ground cinnamon
½ teaspoon ground nutmeg or allspice
1¼ cups (225g) grated carrot
1 cup (110g) chopped walnuts
⅔ cup (110g) raisins*

ICING
*2 cups (200g) flaked coconut
finely grated rind of ½ lemon
3–4 tablespoons confectioner's sugar, to taste
3 tablespoons fresh lemon juice
5–6 tablespoons (75–100ml) hot water
4 tablespoons lightly toasted flaked coconut*

Preheat the oven to 350°F/180°C. Oil a 10in (25cm) ring-
shaped cake tin. Blend the oil and sugar; add the honey
and soy milk, and beat together. Combine the flour,
baking powder, salt, and spices, and add to the oil
mixture. Add the carrots, walnuts, and raisins; mix well
and place in the pan.

Bake in the oven for 55 minutes, or until a skewer
inserted in the thickest part of the cake comes out clean.
Let the cake cool for 5 minutes in the pan, and then turn
out onto a wire rack.

To make the icing, beat together the flaked coconut,
lemon rind, confectioner's sugar, and lemon juice with
enough hot water to give the mixture a spreading
consistency. Spread the icing over the cooled cake, and
then sprinkle evenly with the lightly toasted coconut.
Makes one 10in (25cm) ring-shaped cake.

Fruit Cake

This is a healthy variation on the traditional rich, fruity cake.

Ingredients

18oz (500g) mixed dried fruit,
e.g., raisins, golden raisins, apricots, pears, figs
1½ cups (250g) chopped dates
1 medium apple, cored and chopped
1½ teaspoons cinnamon
seeds of 6 cardamon pods, crushed
½ teaspoon ground ginger
¼ teaspoon ground cloves
2 cups (500ml) orange or apple juice
1¾ cups (200g) plain whole-wheat flour
8 tablespoons (110g) vegetarian shortening
2 cups (200g) roughly ground mixed nuts
2 teaspoons baking powder
pinch of salt
blanched almonds to decorate

FRUIT CAKE

Preheat the oven to 325°F/160°C. Oil a 9in (23cm) round cake pan. Put the dried fruit, dates, chopped apple, cinnamon, cardamon, ginger, cloves, and orange or apple juice into a pan, and bring to a boil, stirring to prevent the mixture from burning. Cook, covered, over low heat until the apple softens and blends with the rest of the fruit (15–20 minutes). Do not allow to dry out.

Mix together the flour, suet, nuts, baking powder, and salt. Add to the cooled fruit mixture, and fold in. Mix well but do not overstir. Pour the mixture into the cake pan and decorate with blanched almonds. Bake in the middle of the oven for 1½–2 hours, or until a skewer inserted in the center comes out clean. Cool on a wire rack.
Makes one 9in (23cm) round cake.

Orange Sauce

Transforms Gingerbread into a dessert

Ingredients

1½ tablespoons arrowroot flour
2 tablespoons lemon juice
1¼ cups (300ml) orange juice
3 teaspoons honey
⅓ teaspoon lemon rind

Place the arrowroot flour and lemon juice in a small pan; stir with a whisk, and place over gentle heat. Add the orange juice and honey, and cook, stirring, until the sauce thickens. Add the lemon rind.
Makes 1¼ cups (300ml).

Gingerbread

A delightful spicy cake to serve at any time, on its own or with tangy Orange Sauce.

Ingredients

¾ cup (180ml) oil
1 cup (225ml) molasses
1½ cups (310ml) yogurt or sour milk
1 teaspoon salt
6 cups (700g) plain whole-wheat flour
½ teaspoon ground cloves
1½ teaspoons cinnamon
1 teaspoon ginger
2 teaspoons baking soda
blanched almonds for decoration (optional)

Preheat the oven to 350°F/180°C. Lightly oil a 8 x 12in (20 x 30cm) rectangular cake tin. Place the oil, molasses, and yogurt or sour milk in a bowl. In another bowl, mix the salt, whole-wheat flour, cloves, cinnamon, ginger, and baking soda. Slowly add together the wet and dry ingredients, and mix thoroughly.

Pour the mixture into the prepared tin, decorate the top with blanched almonds if you wish, and bake in the oven for 40 minutes. The Gingerbread is ready when a skewer inserted in the center comes out clean. Let it cool, and then cut into 2in (5cm) squares. Serve Gingerbread plain or with Orange Sauce (see left).
Makes 24 squares.

FASTING

Fasting, or voluntarily refraining from eating, is one of nature's greatest healing agents, often restoring health when everything else has failed. It gives the whole digestive system a rest, allowing the body to cleanse itself thoroughly, and often removing waste matter and impurities that have accumulated over years.

MENTAL BENEFITS

Fasting is an austerity, one of the five "observances" of the Raja Yoga system. It is practiced to strengthen the mind and the willpower. Just as we can strengthen our muscles by giving them progressively more weight to carry or work to do, so we can also strengthen the mind by giving it increasingly difficult tasks to perform. Fasting will help you develop concentration and mental strength.

Liver benefits from fasting, which is a natural form of cleansing

You may experience slight constipation during a fast

PHYSICAL BENEFITS

Even a one-day fast gives the bowels a rest. The body feels lighter. The whole system is cleansed and given an overhaul. During a fast, the bodily energy that is usually directed toward digestion is available for the repair and healing of the body.

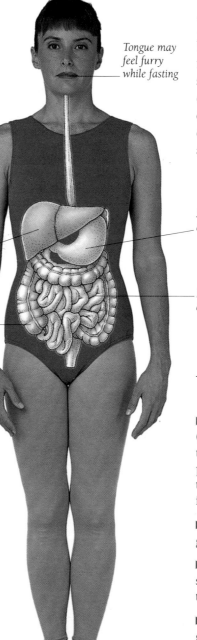

Tongue may feel furry while fasting

Stomach will cease to feel hungry after the third day of the fast

Peristaltic action will slow down or stop in the small intestine

SPIRITUAL BENEFITS

When the body and mind are not taken over three times a day by the vibration of food, they are left free to focus on spiritual matters. All world religions recommend fasting, often with vigil, as a means of strengthening prayer. Many Yogis fast twice a month, on Ekadasi days, 11 days after the new and full moons.

ANAHATA CHAKRA

The energy in the Anahata and Anja chakras can be focused on more easily when body and mind are clear, as they are during a fast.

PLANNING YOUR FASTS

▶ When undertaking a fast for 1–3 days (with the guidance of an expert), pick a time when you can be as quiet as possible, perhaps on the weekend. You may choose to be alone, or with others who are also fasting and will reinforce your resolve.

▶ One day of fasting each week maintains good health and mental resolve.

▶ Weekend fasts are recommended several times per year, especially at the times when the seasons are changing.

▶ Long fasts of a week and more give great spiritual strength. After the third day, hunger will disappear. When you are ready, break the fast gradually (see p.151).

HOW TO FAST

A total fast means abstinence from all food, both liquids and solids. Even juice is not taken during a total fast. Water is not a food. It does not stimulate the appetite and it does not need to be digested. Drinking plenty of water during a fast helps cleanse the body and flush the toxins out of your system.

▶ Do not think of food while you are fasting. Use the time for quiet activity.

▶ Enjoy the time that would have been spent preparing food or eating.

▶ Drink as much water as possible to help flush out the system.

▶ Do asanas; they will help eliminate toxins. Other light exercise, such as walking, is also recommended, but avoid tiring yourself out.

▶ Get as much fresh air as possible, and try to fast in a natural environment.

▶ Be sure to keep your body warm at all times.

▶ Pranayama (see pp.112–13) assists with the cleansing process. Always remember to focus on the exhalation.

▶ Try to practice the Kriyas (see pp.114–15), especially Basti, to cleanse the body.

▶ Bathe frequently, to relax the muscles and assist the skin in its cleansing process.

▶ Rest and relax as much as possible. Try to be quiet and to spend time by yourself whenever you can.

▶ Sometimes, especially when you are new to fasting, you may experience some side effects. If you have a headache or nausea, drink some hot peppermint tea. Do not drink regular tea or coffee.

CAUTION

You should not attempt to fast if you are pregnant, if you have had an eating disorder, or if you suffer from anemia. Consult your doctor if in doubt.

BREAKING THE FAST

It is very important to break your fast correctly. The mind may develop some abnormal cravings for foods. Be careful to resist these impulses. It is best to begin eating slowly.

1 On the first day, eat only raw or stewed fruits. They are easy to digest and will gently restart the peristaltic action in the digestive system.

2 On the second day, you can add a meal of raw vegetable salad. This will act as a broom to sweep out the toxins that have accumulated in the intestines.

3 In addition to the fruits and raw vegetables, include lightly steamed vegetables in your diet on the third day. Do not add any salt or other seasonings to the food.

4 On day four, add grains to your diet of fruits, and raw and lightly steamed vegetables. Grains and vegetables can be combined in a meal.

5 You may return to a well-balanced diet on the fifth day. Try to refrain from unhealthful habits such as coffee, tea, alcohol, and meat.

POSITIVE THINKING & MEDITATION

"Meditation is the royal road to the attainment of freedom, a mysterious ladder that reaches from earth to heaven, darkness to light, mortality to immortality." - Swami Sivananda

WHAT IS POSITIVE THINKING?

To the Yogi, the term "positive thinking" refers to the ability to understand and live in accordance with Vedanta, one of the six main schools of Indian philosophy. The main teachings of Vedanta are to be found in ancient scriptures known as the Upanishads, meaning the "highest knowledge."

VEDANTA PHILOSOPHY

Vedanta teaches that this world is unreal. The only reality is the universal self, or God, which is veiled by Maya (the illusory power). As the veils are lifted, the mind becomes clearer. Unhappiness and fear – even the fear of death – vanish. This state of freedom, or Moksha, is the goal of Yoga. It can be reached by constant enquiry into the nature of things. To assist in this process of enquiry, there are a number of classical stories that act as analogies and help to bring about a true understanding.

*UNAFFECTED BY
THE RAIN*

WATER OFF LOTUS LEAF
Padmapatra Nyaya

When the raindrops land on the lotus leaf, they roll off gently and fall into the water without wetting the leaf.

- INTERPRETATION -

*The leaf is completely unaffected by the rain.
So also, the events of this world have no
ultimate effect on Brahman, or the absolute.
A movie screen offers a similar analogy.
Despite the play of light and shadow upon it,
it remains unchanged and unaffected.*

THE POT AND SPACE
Ghatakasha Nyaya

The space inside a pot is unaffected by the pot. Although the vessel appears to separate the space inside from the outside, this is only an illusion. When the pot is broken, what was inside and what was outside are seen to be the same – they have undergone no change at all.

- INTERPRETATION -

*In the same way, the individual self may
seem to be limited by the mind and body,
but in reality, it is one with the Supreme.*

*THE SPACE DOES
NOT CHANGE WHEN
THE POT BREAKS*

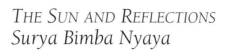

MANY REFLECTIONS, BUT ONLY ONE TRUTH

THE SUN AND REFLECTIONS
Surya Bimba Nyaya

Although the sun may be reflected in an infinite number of vessels, ponds, and lakes, there is still only one sun.

- INTERPRETATION -

Despite the many reflections of Brahman, there is but one reality. It is only Maya, the illusory power of the universe, that causes it to appear as many.

TRY TO PERCEIVE THE ESSENCE

GOLD AND ORNAMENTS
Kanakakundala Nyaya

Although golden ornaments come in diverse shapes and forms, they are all gold in essence. Likewise, there are various kinds of pots – big, small, round, narrow – but all of them are only clay.

- INTERPRETATION -

Although we see the various forms of the world, all is in essence Brahman. There is one underlying reality that appears in all shapes and forms.

ILLUSION MAY MAKE A ROPE APPEAR AS A SNAKE

THE SNAKE AND THE ROPE
Rajjusarpa Nyaya

One evening, as he was walking along an unlit road, a man stepped on a piece of rope that was lying on the ground. In the semidarkness, he mistook the rope for a snake and, imagining that he had been bitten, he screamed in fear. A friend came running with a torch. In the light, the man saw his error, and his fears vanished.

- INTERPRETATION -

When the mind is deluded by Maya (veils of illusion), the world appears to be real. It is only when the light of meditation shines that we truly perceive the reality.

WHY MEDITATE?

LOTUS FLOWER

Meditation is a state of consciousness that can be understood only on a direct, intuitive level. Ordinary experiences are limited by time, space, and the laws of causality, but the meditative state transcends all boundaries. While you meditate, past and future cease to exist. There is only the consciousness of *I am* in the infinite, eternal, *Now*.

WHAT IS HAPPINESS?

Everyone wants to be happy; this is a universal fact. Most people believe that some material object will bring this happiness – money, the perfect spouse, the dream job, a new car, a big house with swimming pool – but in truth the list of what would make you completely happy is never ending. Each "thing" will please only for a short time, until the novelty wears off. As long as you think that happiness will come from something outside yourself, you will never be happy. Happiness, the blissful state, comes from within your own self. Anyone who believes otherwise is like a person wandering in the desert, constantly disappointed by mirages of water and shade. Worldly happiness is equally elusive, always just beyond our grasp. Two famous stories, told below, illustrate the reason why.

Breathing should be regular

Keep the back straight

MEDITATIVE POSE ▷
Sit in a comfortable cross-legged position, with the body straight and the head erect. Breathing must be regular – inhale and exhale for 3 seconds each.

△ SEARCHING FOR SWEETNESS

A man went to visit his guru, and when he arrived he found the teacher sitting in the yard in front of a massive pile of hot chili peppers. The teacher was eating the chilies, one by one. Tears of pain were running down his face and he was sobbing, "This is terrible," over and over. When the man asked his guru why he was doing this, the teacher replied, "I am looking for the sweet one." His actions exemplify the way in which most of us spend our lives. We should know from past experience that "the sweet one" does not exist, but we continue to search for our happiness in external objects. However, the sum total of all the pleasures of the physical world are nothing compared to the blissful state of meditation.

◁ LOOKING IN THE WRONG PLACE

Once, an old woman dropped her needle. A passerby saw her searching in her garden and offered to help. After looking for some time without success, the kindly stranger asked the woman exactly where the needle had fallen. He was amazed to learn that she had dropped it inside the house. "Then why are you looking out here?" he asked. "You will never find it." She replied that her house was too dark, so she was looking outside, where there was more light. Most of us are like that woman. We are looking for our lost happiness where the bright lights are, but it isn't there to be found.

PHYSICAL BENEFITS

Meditation provides a lasting spiritual rest, which must be experienced to be understood. Once you can meditate, the time you normally devote to sleep can gradually be reduced to as little as three hours per night, and you will still feel more rested and peaceful than before. By reducing heart rate and consumption of oxygen, meditation greatly reduces stress levels. It seems that each part of the body, even down to the individual cells, is taught to relax and rejuvenate. Meditation helps to prolong the body's period of growth and cell production, and reduces the decaying process. After the age of 35, our brain cells die off at a rate of 100,000 per day, and they are not replaced, but meditation can reduce this decline, as it changes the vibratory makeup of both the body and the mind. In this way, meditation can prevent or minimize senility.

BRAIN CELLS

Meditation can reduce the rate at which brain cells are lost as we get older.

MENTAL BENEFITS

We each possess vast inner resources of power and knowledge, much of it brought with us from past lives. In meditation, new patterns of thinking come to the surface and develop as we experience a new view of the universe, a vision of unity, happiness, harmony, and inner peace. Negative tendencies vanish, and the mind becomes steady. Meditation brings freedom from fear of death, which is seen as a doorway to a new name and form. People who meditate regularly tend to develop magnetic and dynamic personalities, cheerfulness, powerful speech, lustrous eyes, physical health, and boundless energy. Others draw strength from such people and feel elevated in their presence. Meditation is only possible when all mental modifications (thought waves) have been stilled, and with this comes mental peace.

STATES OF CONSCIOUSNESS

▶ **WAKING STATE**

This is the normal everyday state of awareness. The conscious mind is functioning. You know that you are awake. The intellect is working. You are thinking and reasoning, and you are aware of your physical environment. Time, space, and causality are in full control in the waking state.

▶ **DREAM STATE**

Contrary to popular belief, this intermediate state between waking and deep sleep is not a restful state, as mental energy is being expended. The intellect is not functioning, but there remains some awareness of the physical world. Regular asana practice will help you relax at night and enter deep sleep.

▶ **DEEP SLEEP**

When the mind is relaxed it will go into the state known as deep sleep. The mind is blank; there is no awareness of yourself as a separate entity. The ego identity does not exist. There is no awareness of "I am doing..." nor of your physical environment, nor even an awareness of your own being.

▶ **MEDITATION**

As in deep sleep, neither body consciousness nor awareness of an external physical reality exists. Nor do time, space, or causality, but in meditation the awareness is transcendental. It is the continuous flow of one thought of the Supreme, an identification of the individual with the divine.

CHARTING YOUR PROGRESS IN MEDITATION

"An ounce of practice is worth tons of theory." – Swami Sivananda

▶ Do not abruptly change your way of life. Begin to evolve bit by bit, thus developing your willpower.

▶ Keep a spiritual diary; it may prove to be an eye-opener. It is a simple practical aid to help you to be regular in your practice and to make the most of limited time available.

▶ Make a daily routine and stick to it.

▶ Nightly, just before going to bed, review what you have done that day. Keep the diary for six months and compare your progress.

▶ Remember that regularity and sincerity are the most important secrets to success.

▶ Only you can evaluate whether you are making progress. There are no objective tests or guidelines. No one else can tell you this; it is completely subjective.

▶ Do your body and mind seem to be shedding a kind of dullness or heaviness?

▶ Do you feel more peaceful, more happy with yourself, and less prone to emotional outbursts? Are serenity of mind and a sense of deep-seated contentment starting to manifest themselves?

HOW TO MEDITATE

Meditation is a natural state of consciousness that isn't
learned, any more than you learn to sleep. When the mind becomes
one-pointed and steady, it will naturally go beyond the normal mundane
awareness into the state referred to as meditation.

REGULARITY IS THE KEY

For effective practice of meditation, regularity of time, place, and
practice are most important, since they condition the mind to
focus its energies. The mind seems to be particularly active when
you try to concentrate, but just as any habit can be established
through constant practice, so the mind can be conditioned to
focus more quickly once regularity is established. The steps on
the opposite page will help you attain the goal of meditation.

SITTING POSITION ▷

When you sit for meditation, it is best to be facing
either north or east to take advantage of the magnetic
currents of the earth. Come into a comfortable,
steady cross-legged position (see p.17), with the
spine and neck erect. Metabolism, brain waves, and
breathing all slow down during sitting.

CUPPED HANDS
If you find it more comfortable,
cup the right hand in the left,
with the palms upward.

CLASPED HANDS
Alternatively, you may wish to
clasp the hands by loosely
interlocking the fingers.

NATURE OF MIND

The mind naturally tends
to jump and move about
constantly. Ancient Yogic
scriptures noted that it
can seem more difficult to
control the mind than it is
to control the wind. Yogis
have therefore developed
a whole range of practical
aids and techniques that
will help you in your
attempts at meditation.

Head should be
held erect

Straight back
allows the
energy to move
up the spine

Breathing
should be slow
and steady

Triangular base
helps to contain
the energy

Hands can be
held in Chin
Mudra

Legs can be in a
simple cross-
legged position

1 CHOOSE AN AREA IN YOUR HOME to be used only for meditation. This can be a separate meditation room, or part of a room that is not used for any other purpose. As a focal point, set up an altar with images of your chosen inspirational figure or symbol. This could be a representation of God, in some form, or of your teacher. A cushion or mat will make you more comfortable. With regular practice, your meditation space will become charged with a powerful positive energy.

SUNRISE IS A GOOD TIME TO MEDITATE

2 SET ASIDE A SPECIFIC TIME of day for meditation. The most effective times are dawn and dusk, when the atmosphere is charged with especially uplifting spiritual energy, so try to practice first thing in the morning or last thing at night. Meditation comes most easily in the clear hours of the morning, when the world is at peace and the mind is rested and has not yet engaged itself in its daily activities.

3 BEGIN BY SITTING for meditation for 20 minutes daily; gradually increase your time to one hour. For this period you will try to forget about the past, the present, and the future. Request the mind to be quiet, but do not force the mind, as this creates unnecessary tension. At first you will probably find that your mind wanders and jumps around. Allow it to do so. Eventually it will concentrate, along with the concentration of prana. Try to develop the attitude of a silent witness, watching the activity of your mind, but without becoming involved with it.

MEDITATE AT FIRST FOR 20 MINUTES

PROGRESS TO 60 MINUTES

4 CONSCIOUSLY REGULATE THE BREATH. Begin with a few minutes of deep breathing to bring a fresh supply of oxygen to the brain. Then gradually slow the breath, keeping it rhythmic. Inhale for 3 seconds and exhale for 3 seconds. Controlling the breath regulates the flow of prana within the body.

5 WITHDRAW YOUR ATTENTION from all outside objects. In meditation, all awareness of the physical world ceases. Rather than allowing the eyes to see, or the ears to hear, withdraw the mental energy from them, so that the stimuli from the outside world do not impinge upon the mind. Close your eyes and focus your attention inward. Choosing an internal point of concentration will help you to do this.

6 SELECT A POINT OF CONCENTRATION within yourself. This can be the Ajna chakra, between the eyebrows, for those who are predominantly intellectual, or the Anahata chakra, the heart center, for those whose nature is more emotional. Once you have chosen a point, always use the same one in your meditation practice. You should not change your point of focus.

AJNA CHAKRA

ANAHATA CHAKRA

7 FOCUS THE MIND on a neutral or uplifting object or sound, such as a mantra, and hold this at the chosen point of concentration. It is impossible to empty the mind, but this will give the mind something positive on which to concentrate. If you are using a mantra, repeat it mentally as you breathe in and as you breathe out. Mental repetition is stronger and more subtle. If you do not have a personal mantra, you can use "Om". Once you have chosen a mantra, do not change it.

OM SYMBOL

8 REGULAR REPETITION of a mantra will purify the mind. After a time, the sound merges with thought, leaving no awareness of external meaning. Vocal repetition progresses through mental repetition to telepathic language, and then to pure thought or the transcendental state.

9 WHEN YOU FIRST enter the state of transcendental bliss, a sense of duality remains. Ego-consciousness will still be there, and subject and object still exist in a subtle form. With practice, duality disappears and the super-conscious state of Samadhi is reached.

COUNTING MANTRAS USING MALA BEADS

10 IN SAMADHI, you rest in a state of transcendental bliss in which the knower, knowledge, and the known become one. This is the superconscious experience of the absolute reached by mystics and saints of all faiths and persuasions.

MEDITATION TOOLS

Meditation is best practiced somewhere quiet and free from distractions, and in a moderate temperature. This may be in your home or in a natural setting. Aside from these basics, you need little more than the proper attitude and a keen desire to expand your inner horizons.

SACRED SPACE

The place in which you meditate should be kept clean and neat. Place fresh flowers in it daily. An altar, covered with a clean cloth, will act as a focus for your meditation. An oil lamp or candle may be kept burning to purify the environment, or lit when you sit for your practice. Add some uplifting pictures, statues, or symbols that have meaning for you.

COMFORTABLE SEAT
Arrange a place to sit facing the altar, using a low cushion or mat. A cushion under the buttocks will relieve any possible strain on the knees.

INCENSE
Burn soothing incense to help calm the mind when you sit for meditation. Sandalwood and frankincense have this effect.

CANDLE OR OIL LAMP
By lighting an oil lamp or a candle, you are symbolizing your readiness to tune yourself to the inner light.

JAPA MALA
Repetitions of mantras, or japa, may be counted using a string of 108 mala beads. Hold them in the right hand and count them between the thumb and middle fingers (not the index finger, as it symbolizes the ego).

FRESH FLOWERS
The meditation area should be kept clean and sattvic (pure). A bouquet of fresh flowers placed on the altar every day will inspire and uplift the mind, encouraging a mood that is conducive to meditation.

CHRIST
A picture of your conception of God, be it Christ, Krishna, or someone else, or a symbol of your religious belief, personalizes your practice and helps create an atmosphere in which the mind can tune to higher things.

THE TEACHER
Just as you need a flame to light a candle, so you need a teacher to provide the basic techniques and principles for you to begin your practice. A portrait will remind you of the teachings and help to focus your mind.

MANTRAS AS MENTAL TOOLS

The word "mantra" is derived from the Sanskrit words "manas," meaning mind, and "tra," meaning to take across or to go beyond. A mantra is a mystical symbol encased in a sound structure, a mental tool that, through repetition, helps the mind in its quest to transcend its normal limitations. Once you have chosen a mantra, you should never change it. Eight mantras are described here, and some are shown with images and models of the particular Hindu gods with which they are associated. All of these gods represent aspects of the one god that dwells in all.

THE ALTAR
You may choose to place a combination of any of the elements shown here on your altar. If you don't like symbols, pictures, or statues at all, simply place a clean cloth and some flowers on a low table and use this simple altar as your point of focus.

OM NAMO NARAYANAYA
(Om Na-Mo Naa-Raa-Ya-Na-Ya) This mantra is associated with the god Vishnu, representing the preserving energy that keeps the universe in balance. It is seen as a peace mantra, of particular use at this time, when negative energies seem to be out of control.

OM SRI MAHA LAKSHMYAI NAMAH
(Om Shree Ma-Ha Laksh-MeYay Na-Mah) Lakshmi is seen as God taking the form of the ever-giving Mother. She is the source and giver of all blessings and wealth, especially the blessings of inner peace and spiritual prosperity.

SOHAM
(So-Ham) This is a philosophical, or Vedantic, mantra. The words may be roughly translated as "I am that I am," meaning that no limitations can be put on the divine. Soham is the natural sound of the breath being inhaled and exhaled.

OM
(A-U-M) Om is the highest and most abstract mantra of all. Om is the Shabdabrahman, or the sound by which the universe was created, the ancient name for the "big bang" theory of modern scientists. Om is all sounds, all vibrations, and all mantras together.

OM NAMO BHAGAVATE VASUDEVAYA
(Om Na-Mo Bha-Ga-Va-Tay Vaa-Soo-Dave-Aya) Krishna is seen as the supreme world teacher, as he is the giver of the Bhagavad Gita, *one of the great texts on Yoga.*

OM NAMAH SIVAYA
(Om Na-Mah She-Va-Ya) As Nataraja, the Cosmic Dancer, Siva presides over the constant destruction and re-creation of the universe, the energy that destroys the lower self to allow positive personal growth.

OM GAM GANAPATAYE NAMAH
(Om Gam Ga-Na-Pa-Ta-Yay Na-Mah) Ganapathi is another name for Ganesha, the elephant-headed deity who is revered as the remover of obstacles and bestower of success.

OM SRI DURGAYAI NAMAH
(Om Shree Dur-Ga-Yay Na-Mah) In Durga, we see God as mother. She is the divine protector. In Her arms She holds all the powers of the Universe. She rides a lion, symbolizing the forces of nature.

GLOSSARY

Entries indicated in *italics* are also listed individually within the glossary

AJNA CHAKRA The sixth *chakra*, located at the point between the eyebrows and often referred to as the "third eye."

ANAHATA CHAKRA The fourth *chakra*, located at the heart center.

ASANA Physical Yogic exercise, practiced to improve the control of the mind and body. In *Sanskrit*, this word means posture or position.

ASHTANGA YOGA Another name for *Raja Yoga*, meaning 8-limbed or 8-stepped.

ASTRAL BODY The subtle body, containing the *prana*, mind, intellect, and emotions.

BASTI Cleansing of the colon, or lower digestive tract. One of the six *Kriyas*.

BHAGAVAD GITA The Hindu scripture that provides the philosophical basis of Yoga.

BHAKTI YOGA The Yogic path of devotion. Includes such practices as chanting and prayer, which sublimate the emotions and channel them into devotion.

CAUSAL BODY The most subtle of the three bodies, also known as the seed body. Contains the karmic (see *karma*) blueprint that determines the person you are.

CERVICAL REGION The top seven vertebrae of the spine, which support your head.

CHAKRAS The seven energy centers in the *astral body* where many *nadis*, or astral nerves, come together. They correspond to the nerve plexuses located along the spine in the physical body.

CHIN MUDRA The hand position made by joining the thumb and index finger. (See *Mudra* for further explanation.)

DHAUTI A purifying exercise to cleanse the upper digestive tract (mouth, esophagus, and stomach). One of the six *Kriyas*.

DIAPHRAGM The flat muscular sheet below the rib cage. Separates the chest cavity from the abdominal cavity. Its movement controls breathing.

EKADASI Many Yogis use a lunar calendar to decide which days are best for fasting. Ekadasi days, 11 days after the full moon and 11 days after the new moon, are considered to be the most beneficial days.

GERUNDA SAMHITA One of the foremost ancient texts describing *Hatha Yoga*.

GUNAS The three qualities of Nature: *sattva*, *rajas*, and *tamas*. According to Yogic philosophy, everything is made up of the gunas in different proportions.

HATHA YOGA The word "Hatha" is made up of the *Sanskrit* syllables "ha" (sun) and "tha" (moon). Hatha Yoga indicates the union of these two opposites. It is the path of Yoga that deals primarily with the physical body, but in addition to *asanas* and *pranayama* it includes all the other practices of Raja Yoga, such as ethical behavior and *meditation*.

HATHA YOGA PRADIPIKA One of the foremost ancient texts on Hatha Yoga, written by the great Yogi Swatmarama.

IDA One of the three main meridians in the astral body. The subtle channel to the left of the *Sushumna*, through which *prana* passes for about half of the day.

JAPA Repetition of a *mantra*

JNANA YOGA One of the four main paths of Yoga, Jnana Yoga is the intellectual or philosophical approach. The practice of Jnana Yoga usually demands the study of the *Vedanta* philosophy of the *Upanishads*.

KAPALABHATI An exercise involving rapid abdominal breathing that cleanses the respiratory tract. One of the six *Kriyas*.

KARMA The literal translation of this *Sanskrit* word means "action," which is understood also to include the reaction. Karma operates through the law of cause and effect, meaning that everything happening to you is the effect of your past actions in this life or a past life.

KARMA YOGA The path of selfless service. By performing actions without wanting reward or payment, the Yogi tries to free him- or herself from the seemingly endless wheel of births and deaths.

KRIYAS The set of six purification exercises: *Neti, Nauli, Dhauti, Basti, Kapalabhati,* and *Tratak*.

KUNDALINI The primordial cosmic energy, or *Shakti*, dormant within each individual.

LUMBAR REGION The lumbar group in the lower back. Consists of five *vertebrae*, and supports most of your body weight.

MALA A string of 108 beads; it is a powerful tool to help focus the mind for meditation.

MANIPURA CHAKRA The third *chakra*, corresponding to the solar plexus.

MANTRA A mystical syllable, word, or phrase used to focus the mind during *meditation*. Can be repeated mentally or out loud. *Om* is the best known mantra.

MAYA The illusory power of the divine. Yogis say that the whole world is a play of Maya, a divine illusion.

MEDITATION The state of consciousness characterized by stillness and inner calm. The ultimate goal is the attainment of supreme spiritual peace.

MUDRA A hand position that channels the *prana* in specific directions.

MULADHARA CHAKRA The lowest *chakra*, located at the base of the spine.

NADIS In Yogic theory, there are about 72,000 nadis or subtle tubes in the *astral body*. They equate to the acupuncture meridians. The three most important are the *Ida, Pingala,* and *Sushumna.*

NAULI One of the six *Kriyas*, involving a strong churning of the abdomen.

NETI A *Kriya*, or cleansing exercise, for the nose and sinus cavities.

OJAS SHAKTI Spiritual energy.

OM The sacred monosyllable, often written as "Aum," that symbolizes God as the absolute. Om is the universal *mantra,* containing all other mantras and sounds.

PINGALA One of the three most important *nadis*, or astral nerves, located to the right of the *Sushumna.* Corresponds to the right sympathetic nerve in the physical body.

PRANA The vital energy or life force. Flows through the *astral body* in the *nadis.*

PRANAYAMA Yogic breathing exercises designed for cleansing and strengthening the mind and body. In the more advanced stages, pranayama enables the practitioner to control the flow of *prana,* or vital energy, in the body.

RAJA YOGA The "royal" path of Yoga, the branch applying mainly to mental control. *Raja Yoga* is also seen as the scientific or step-by-step approach, hence it is also referred to as *Ashtanga Yoga.*

RAJAS The quality of overactivity and passion – one of the three *gunas.* Yogis try to avoid food, situations, and conditions that are rajasic.

SACRAL REGION These five vertebrae make up the lowest region of the spine. They are fused to form a single bone, which is part of the pelvic girdle.

SADHANA Spiritual practice.

SAHASRARA CHAKRA Symbolized by a thousand-petaled lotus, this is the seventh *chakra*, or the highest energy center in the body. It is here that the Yogi unites the individual self with God.

SAMADHI The superconscious state in which all ego identity of the meditator is gone. One experiences absolute bliss.

SAMSKARA A subtle impression of everything that has happened to the individual in this life and all past lives. All Samskaras are stored in the *causal,* or seed, *body* in the form of *karma*, to be worked out when the opportunity arises.

SANSKRIT Often referred to as "Devanagari," the language of the gods, Sanskrit is probably the most ancient of human languages. Yoga uses many Sanskrit terms, as they cannot be exactly translated into English or any other Western language.

SATTVA The quality of lightness and purity – one of the three *gunas*. Practitioners of Yoga try to keep their diet and everything else about their lives as sattvic as possible.

SCIATIC NERVE One of the largest nerves in the back of the leg, running through the buttocks and down the thigh. Sciatica, or inflammation of the sciatic nerve, is a common and very painful condition.

SHAKTI The primordial cosmic energy seen in the personification of the great goddess, or *Kundalini.*

SIVA The divine inspiration of Yoga. Most of the classical treatises of *Hatha Yoga* are in the form of an exposition by Siva, the great Yogi, to his wife Parvati.

SOLAR PLEXUS The network of nerves that lies just behind the stomach.

SUSHUMNA The most important of all 72,000 *nadis*. The *prana* is in the Sushumna only when you are meditating. One of the benefits of the Alternate Nostril Breathing exercise is that it helps to bring the *prana* into the Sushumna.

SWADHISHTANA CHAKRA The second energy center on the *Sushumna*, it is located in the genital region.

TAMAS The quality of lethargy, inertia, and laziness. Yogis try to avoid food, situations, and conditions that are tamasic.

THORACIC REGION These are the 12 *vertebrae* behind the chest area, to which the ribs are connected. This part of the spine tends to be rather rigid.

TRANSCENDENTAL The quality of going beyond the limitations of the mind. All *meditation* is transcendental by nature.

TRATAK One of the six purificatory exercises, or *Kriyas*, Tratak stimulates a powerful cleansing of the eye, sinus, and forehead region.

UPANISHADS Ancient *Sanskrit* scriptures containing the central tenets of *Vedanta* philosophy.

VAIRAGYA Dispassion. This is essential for any real *Sadhana* to be practiced. Vairagya follows from the acquisition of *Viveka,* or discrimination.

VEDANTA Advaita Vedanta, or complete monistic philosophy. One of the six major schools of Hindu philosophy. Its main exponent was the ninth-century sage, philosopher, and poet Adi Sankaracharya.

VERTEBRAE The 24 bones that form the spinal column. There are, starting from the top, seven cervical, 12 thoracic, and five lumbar vertebrae, plus the sacrum and the coccyx.

VISHNU MUDRA The hand position used in the Alternate Nostril Breathing exercise. (See also *mudra.*)

VISHUDDHA CHAKRA The fifth energy center in the *astral body*, this *chakra* is located at the base of the throat.

VIVEKA Spiritual discrimination. The ability to differentiate between what is real and what is unreal, what is permanent and what is changing.

USEFUL ADDRESSES

AUSTRALIA
Sivananda Yoga Vedanta Centre
40 Ninth Avenue
Katoomba, NSW 2780
Tel: (047) 823245

AUSTRIA
Sivananda Yoga Vedanta Zentrum
Rechte Wienzeile 29-3-9
A-1040 Vienna
Tel: (01) 586-3453

BAHAMAS
Sivananda Ashram Yoga Retreat
P.O. Box N7550, Nassau
Tel: (809) 363-2902

CANADA
Sivananda Yoga Vedanta Centre
5178 St. Lawrence Blvd
Montreal, Quebec H2T 1R8
Tel: (514) 279-3545

Sivananda Yoga Vedanta Centre
77 Harbord Street
Toronto, Ontario M5S 1G4
Tel: (416) 966-9642

Sivananda Ashram Yoga Camp
8th Avenue, Val Morin
Quebec JOT 2RO
Tel: (819) 322-3226

FRANCE
Centre de Yoga Sivananda Vedanta
123 Boul. Sebastopol
F-75002 Paris
Tel: (01) 40-26-77-49

GERMANY
Sivananda Yoga Vedanta Zentrum
Steinheilstr. 1
D-80333 Munich
Tel: (089) 52-44-76 / 52-17-35

Sivananda Yoga Vedanta Zentrum
Heilbronnerstr. 21
D-10779 Berlin
Tel: (030) 211-5865

INDIA
Sivananda Yoga Vedanta Nataraja Centre
52 Community Centre, East of Kailash
New Delhi 110 065
Tel: (011) 644-3697

Sivananda Yoga Vedanta Centre
37/1929, West Fort, Airport Road
Trivandrum, Kerala 695 023
Tel: (0471) 450-942

Sivananda Yoga Vedanta
    Dhanwanthari Ashram
P.O. Neyyar Dam
Thiruvanthapuram Dt.
Kerala 695 576
Tel: (047254) 493

Sivananda Yoga Vedanta Centre
2 Ranjit Road, Kotturpuram
Madras 600 085 T.N.
Tel: (044) 418-431

ISRAEL
Sivananda Yoga Vedanta Centre
6 Lateris St.
Tel Aviv 64166
Tel: (03) 691-6793

SPAIN
Centro de Yoga Sivananda Vedanta
Calle Juan Bravo 62-7-A
S-28006 Madrid
Tel: (01) 402-7467

SWITZERLAND
Centre de Yoga Sivananda Vedanta
1 Rue des Minoteries
CH-1205 Geneva
Tel: (022) 328-0328

URUGUAY
Asociación de Yoga Sivananda
Acevedo Diaz 1523
11200 Montevideo
Tel: (02) 41-09-29

UNITED KINGDOM
Sivananda Yoga Vedanta Centre
51 Felsham Road
London SW15 1AZ
Tel: (0181) 780-0160

UNITED STATES
Sivananda Yoga Vedanta Center
243 West 24th Street
New York, NY 10011
Tel: (212) 255-4560

Sivananda Yoga Vedanta Center
1200 Arguella Blvd.
San Francisco, CA 94122
Tel: (415) 681-2731

Sivananda Yoga Vedanta Center
1246 Bryn Mawr
Chicago, IL 60660
Tel: (312) 878-7771

Sivananda Yoga Vedanta Center
1746 Abbot Kinney Blvd.
Venice, CA 90291
Tel: (310) 822-9642

Sivananda Ashram Yoga Ranch Colony
P.O. Box 195, Budd Road
Woodbourne, NY 12788
Tel: (914) 434-9242

Sivananda Ashram Yoga Farm
Comp. 8
14651 Ballantree Lane,
Grass Valley, CA 9594
Tel: (916) 272-9322

ACKNOWLEDGMENTS

AUTHOR'S CREDITS

Swami Saradananda would like to thank Swami Sadasivananda, and all the staff of the Sivananda Yoga Vedanta Centre, London, for their help and advice; Amba, Radhika, and Shambu for their skill and enthusiasm in demonstrating the Yoga techniques; Shakti Warwick in New York; Shambavi and Jagatamba of the Sivananda Ashram Yoga Camp in Val Morin, Quebec, Canada; and Swami Premananda in London, for their help with the recipes.

PUBLISHER'S CREDITS

The publisher would like to thank Hilary Bird for the index, Ingrid Nilsson for picture research, Wayne Strudwick for design assistance, and Julie Whitaker for proofreading.

Special thanks to the staff of the Sivananda Yoga Vedanta Centre in London for their enthusiastic cooperation throughout the project and for their kind hospitality (and above all for the cookies!).

ILLUSTRATORS

Joanna Cameron 29, 37, 39, 49, 53, 65, 69, 73, 85, 89, 91, 99, 101; Simone End 125; Rodney Shackell 1, 3, 7, 9, 10, 68, 109 top left, 110, 111 center right, 124, 126 bottom left, 127, 150 bottom left, 154-5, 156, 159; Colin Walton 8–9, 126 bottom right; John Woodcock; 38, 40, 48, 60, 63, 64, 72, 76, 82, 88, 90, 94.

MODEL PHOTOGRAPHY

PHOTOGRAPHERS Andy Crawford and Steve Gorton
MODELS Amba (Anna Winkler), Radhika Chaitanya, Shambu (Manoj Bulsara)
COSTUMES Beverley Vas at Splitz Dancewear.
Thanks also to Pineapple, 6A Langley Street, London WC2H 9JA
HAIR AND MAKEUP Bettina Graham
PODIATRIST Aihun Charles

FOOD PHOTOGRAPHY

PHOTOGRAPHER Clive Streeter
HOME ECONOMIST Poppy Body
RECIPE TESTING Carol Tennant
ART DIRECTION Ann Thompson
ADDITIONAL PHOTOGRAPHY Colin Walton

ALL OTHER PHOTOGRAPHY BY

Jane Burton, Geoff Dann, Steve Gorton, Frank Greenaway, Chas Howson, Dave King, Steven Oliver, Jane Stockman, Colin Walton, and Jerry Young, with the exception of the following: – Biofotos / Heather Angel 156 top left; Bruce Coleman 116–7 / Jules Cowan 12–13; Ecoscene / Sally Morgan 127 top center; Robert Harding Picture Library 152–3; Holt Studios 127 top left; Image Bank 118 bottom left / G&M David de Lossy 151 bottom left / Frank Whitney 159 center left; Images Colour Library 111 top left; Pictor 119 center left; Pictures Colour Library 106–7; Science Photo Library 109 top right / Dr Tony Brain 108 bottom left / CNRI 157 top left; Tony Stone / Tony Page 121 bottom right / Charles Thatcher 119 center right; Zefa Pictures 109 bottom left, 110 left, 118 bottom right, 122–3.